CROSS THAT BRIDGE...
BEFORE YOU GET THERE

Charlie Pitts

Lody !
It has been a,
pleasure getting to
know you over the
years ! Enjoy the
read. Charlie Pitts
11-1-13

CONTENTS

DEDICATION

Sir Isaac Newton said, "If I have seen further it is by standing on the shoulders of giants." I am who I am because of those who chose to mentor and invest in me. Those who have invested in me have invested in this book. They have helped me to **Cross Those Bridges…BEFORE I Got There**. It is my honor to dedicate this book to those giants.

Jesus Christ: Thank You for paying the ultimate price and for paying a debt that I could not pay.

Pastors Alan & Joy Clayton, Senior Pastors of the Ark Church, Conroe, Texas: Thank you, Pastors, for turning me on to Leadership Books and for helping me to understand the value of serving. Thank you both for seeing me through the tough times.

Karen Denise Pitts, my wife and partner: Thank you, Sweetheart, for encouraging me to pursue my dreams and for putting up with my hearing loss.

Mom and Dad, Charles and Iris Pitts: Dad, thanks for teaching me the value of honesty, hard work and taking pride in everything I do. Thanks for reaching out to me as teen and validating my worth. Mom, thanks for always believing in me and for all your prayers that kept me safe during my foolish teen years.

Richard E. Moore: Dick, it was a pleasure to work with you for over 30 years. Thanks for taking the time to mentor me.

Pamela McCown: Madame Past International Director for Toastmasters International, thank you for believing in me, pushing me, encouraging me, and for all of your mentoring.

PREFACE

My pursuit of Success has lead me to read hundreds of books, and I have listened to a truckload of tapes. And while I am a product of many of these great authors and teachers, time and time again, I find myself in the forest of fads, formulas, and fiction—and often I could not see the forest for the fads. Many of the books I tried to follow contain 10 chapters consisting of 10 steps each. At the end of the day, I was left with 100 steps to remember! That just set me—and any other reader—up for failure.

What I discovered through personal experience is that to achieve **True Success**, the effort has to be sustainable. This does not come by applying formulas, following fads, or selling out to fiction. And there are no short cuts. My journey is based on three pillars that create Sustainable Confidence, which in turn results in Sustainable Success. Have you ever hit a homerun but lacked the confidence to believe you could repeat it? The journey that I endorse provides the confidence to Sustain Success and to repeat that Success in multiple arenas.

I started my journey in childhood with low self-esteem and had to rely on external confidence builders, such as football and boxing—but the confidence never lasted. I was fortunate to discover the three pillars outlined in this book, because they truly changed my life. These three pillars have aided me in chairing organizations such as the Energy Rubber Group, serving as the Distinguished District 56 Governor, 2009/2010 for Toastmasters International, moving from engineering into sales, and exceeding sales goals and developing business overseas.

With a track record of achieving <u>Sustainable Success</u>, it is time to share the golden nuggets I've gleaned through my experience. I must admit that I still have so much more to learn. We never arrive; we just hit a different plateau. These principles have been refined in the smelting pot of my own life. Thomas Paine said, "What we obtain too cheaply, we esteem too lightly. It is only dearness that gives a thing its value."

The lessons that my successes and failures have taught me also come with tremendous expense—blood, sweat, tears, embarrassment, humiliation, and, at times, devastation. It is my honor to share these valuable principles that have emerged from beneath the dross—saving you time and hardship.

<u>Why this book?</u> The principles discussed in this book focus on three pillars that can be practiced now. There are not 100 steps. There is no investment but your time and dedication. Just strengthening one pillar will yield substantial results. Rolling out all three will lay a solid foundation of confidence, revolutionize your effectiveness and impact, and most of all, you will enjoy <u>Sustainable Success.</u>

HOW TO USE THIS BOOK

This book is packed with rich Quotes and Golden Nuggets.

> *"Quotes are in big black boxes." Charlie Pitts*

Golden Nuggets: Are bold and italicized.

These quotes and Golden Nuggets are reprinted at the back of each chapter for easy reference.

Also located at the back of each chapter is a notes page. To get the most out of this book, underline important concepts. Then make a reference to those important and significant nuggets on your notes page. And be sure to reference your note with a page number—this will allow you to quickly refer back to key points.

Example:

Notes Page:

Reference	Page No.
Equation for Success	Page 18
Success rises and falls….	Page 18

INTRODUCTION:

Cross That Bridge...BEFORE You Get There provides a pathway to Sustainable Success. I used to have a recurring dream that I was able fly. I had the most wonderful feeling when I lifted my arms, eased into the air, and soared high above the ground. It was effortless, at least until I realized I wasn't actually able to fly. Then came the rapid decent. I could fly but I was unable to sustain flight. I am convinced that our frustrations, worries and insecurities play out in our dreams— and my worry was that while I could achieve a goal, I wouldn't be able to sustain it.

When our Success is built on a shaky foundation rather than on solid, confidence-building principles, there will always be doubt, insecurity, and inadequacies. And doubt always causes us to lose altitude. While in flight is the worst time to lose confidence in our ability to fly.

As I began to live by the concepts described in this book, my dreams changed. For the first time, I was able to sustain flight, although I did have a bit of trouble with turns. It's amazing to me that the confidence gained from practicing solid principles was also manifested in my dreams. I have achieved tremendous Success by **Crossing That Bridge...BEFORE I Get There**. As I've said, this book is simple and has only three principles, which I call the pillars of Preparation:

Planning: Creating a Plan

Picturing: Painting the Picture of Success

Purpose: Finding or Creating Purpose

Well, let's take the journey. Let's prepare for the bridge.

FOREWORD

I like this book! It contains simple principles that anyone can utilize, and Charlie Pitts is living proof that these principles work.

Charlie and I go back over 27 years. He has been an invaluable source of counsel, support, and friendship as he helped me launch two separate ministries. But when he came to me 16 years ago with the idea of going into sales, inwardly I winced. I did not think that Charlie had the "personality" for sales. Having spent 15 years in that field I assumed that I was a good gauge of his potential. What I could not gauge was Charlie's willingness to prepare to win. The principles of planning, picturing, and purpose he explains in this book, elevated him to promotion after promotion, and I watched as his income increased five-fold in that 16-year period. In hindsight, I am really glad I kept my mouth shut!

If you ever get a chance to meet Charlie Pitts you will like him! He is as genuine and grounded as they come. During his rise to success after success he still showed up every Sunday to lead one of our most challenging volunteer positions in the church—our First Touch parking lot ministry. A parking lot in the south Texas summer would test the commitment of a saint!

But what also makes Charlie Pitts unique is his intense desire to help people coupled with his belief that anyone can elevate his or her life and find success. With his own rise out of a modest start Charlie has learned and applied the principles he outlines in *Cross That Bridge…BEFORE You Get There*. He believes these principles will work for you, and he is right. As his pastor I wish I had more men like Charlie Pitts. As an observer of his success I am honored to recommend him and this book to you. For some it will stir up things you have let slip, for others it will provide an excellent template to change and acquire Sustainable Success. Read it and learn to cross that bridge before you get there and then enjoy the benefits on the other side.

All the best,

Alan Clayton

Senior Pastor

The Ark Church

Conroe, Texas

REVIEWS

"Charlie Pitts is the real deal, the genuine article, a person who says what he means and means what he says. I have heard many of the stories and concepts over the years and have been a party to many interesting conversations with Charlie.

As I read this book, I felt as if I was hearing Charlie's voice. If you want to set out on a path to personal improvement and aspire to a higher level of success, then read this book. I enjoyed reading this outline of how planning, painting visual images of success, and living with a purpose can change your life.

It is good to be reminded of these concepts. They truly are the building blocks of any successful endeavor."

—Pamela McCown, DTM TOASTMASTERS INTERNATIONAL DIRECTOR 2009-2011

"Not too many people get 'authentic connection with people' and 'the art of communication' better than Charlie Pitts. I have had the pleasure of knowing him as a key volunteer, board member, and friend for longer than either he or I would care to admit. Charlie speaks from his heart, his character, and his own life experience and knows full well the power of 'crossing that bridge before you get there.'

You will be inspired and challenged from Charlie's practical application to life and business. Drawing on his wealth of experience as a leader, sales executive, and communicator you will definitely make a solid investment by reading and applying the following pages… Enjoy."

—Phillip Moore, Executive Pastor, The Ark Church, Conroe, TX

"One day, I heard Charlie Pitts give a short speech. After it, I was so inspired that I jumped up and hurried to where he was talking to a group of people. I told him, 'Charlie, I want to be on your leadership team. I don't care which role, I'll fill any position you need. That began my journey in Toastmasters International district leadership, a journey that has enriched my life. Charlie is one of my key mentors. By reading this book, you, too, will be inspired to step into leadership, and you will have tools to carry with you in your journey. You will get to know Charlie, and like me, you will count yourself lucky."

—Karen G. Blake, Distinguished Toastmaster, Past Distinguished District 56 Governor – Toastmasters International

"Regardless of your level of accomplishment, this book will give you a firestorm of wisdom. Unlike the plethora of most modern 'improvement' books that have schemes, tactics, and tricks, this is one that focuses on methodology for refinement of the platinum standard of success...character. This book is more like scripture and less like Success magazine. The author has also made it more like a workbook than a story. If you are looking for a pragmatic read that will have lasting impact on what matters most in achieving your destiny and purpose, this is a great read."

—Mark Faust, Author, Speaker, and Founder of Echelon Management International

"I have known Charlie for some time; where he comes from they might call it "a coon's age." Charlie and I met in 1996 while serving at The Ark Church in Conroe, Texas.

At the time we met I don't think either of us knew the journey of leadership, personal growth and communication we were headed for. During our first few years at The Ark, we were exposed to some very strong examples like John Maxwell, Toastmasters, and our Pastor, Alan Clayton, who in his own right is one of the finest leaders I know. These principles and examples stretched and shaped both of us.

When you serve alongside someone for any length of time, you get to know what they are really made of; their true character is revealed.

Having volunteered with Charlie, I have come to know the strength of his desire to serve others to the best of his ability and continually grow spiritually and personally.

I have also seen first-hand the quality of Charlie's character, which is rock solid.

As you read his words, you can rest assured they come from someone who truly has your best interest and desire for you to be the best you can be at heart."

—Vic Tarasik, CEO Vic's Precision Automotive

CHAPTER 1

SUSTAINABLE SUCCESS

All the neighborhood kids were really mad at me. They said I undercut them. At the age of 12, my lawn business was flourishing, and I was taking business away from the other boys in the neighborhood on a regular basis.

I started mowing lawns because I wanted a mini-bike, so my dad fixed me up with a lawn mower, a gas can, clippers, and a broom. I had two pieces of equipment more than my competitors. You see, they only mowed. They did not clip the grass around the sidewalks or air conditioners. They did not sweep the sidewalks either. In addition to doing an excellent job, I charged less. My competitors charged $2.00 and I charged $1.25. I was not only known as the cheapest one around, I was also known for doing excellent work. As a result, my business was thriving!

My competition did not understand that I wasn't just cheaper, I also offered more services for my $1.25 than they did for $2.00. That summer I learned the value of doing excellent work and started my journey of many successes. For me at 12, Success was a mini bike. (And I did achieve my goal.)

Now as an adult and a career man, I have learned that I can charge for the additional value. I should have been charging more than my competitors.

I was initially timid about asking for the business, but after I did an excellent job and received great feedback from my customers, I gained confidence and courage. This was a successful venture for me, but I still had lessons to learn. At the age of 15, I drove from Pearl, Mississippi, to Kountze, Texas (without a license), to spend the summer with my grandfather, Papa C.A. He and I planted a large vegetable garden that summer. While he was working during the day, I used the tractor to break up the ground. He came home early one day to find me struggling. There was a low, wet area, and this was a problem. But it was made worse by the large roots that would stick the tractor. This was also somewhat dangerous. When a tractor gets stuck, it has enough torque to pull the front end up and can flip. I had to be quick on the clutch to avoid the tractor rolling over backwards and me being trapped under the machine.

Papa C.A. saw me struggling, and I can remember him shouting at me, "Don't let that tractor work you. You work that tractor!" His advice was fine and dandy, but in order to keep the tractor from working me, I needed more experience. However, the concept of working smarter as opposed to harder stayed with me.

It was during my football days that this concept actually came to life. I played football throughout my grade school and high school years. As an offensive lineman, I was taught to fire off the line as soon as the ball is snapped; however, this does not work when you are 140 pounds and are matched up with a 250-pound defensive lineman. I had a fast growth spurt from the fifth through the seventh grades and was taller than my teammates. I played lineman, but as I got older, my teammates began to grow larger than me.

I was so much faster than my larger opponents that when I fired off the line, I usually caught my opponent still in his stance. My larger opponent had the better position and would brush me aside. I learned to fire off the line with my initial step and offer a slight hesitation. My opponents would immediately raise up, which allowed me to catch them at the waist and to drive them out of the lane. I could not manhandle my opponents, but I was able to outsmart them.

This was actually a turning point in my life. I now understood the lesson Papa C.A. was attempting to teach me. I learned that I could compensate for my shortcomings with other resources available and still create the win!

From humble beginnings, my journey has provided me opportunities beyond my wildest dreams. As I look back, it was those simple lessons that I learned as a child along with the new lessons learned as an adult that have contributed to my successes.

My accomplishments include working as an engineer for 18 years and working as a salesman for 14 years. Positions held include Engineering Manager, VP of Sales & Marketing, and, currently, Business Development Manager–Asia Pacific. My responsibilities are to develop the business in Asia Pacific and to find and assist in acquisitions. In 2009/2010, I served as the Chair of the Energy Rubber Group in the Gulf Coast Region, and at the same time, I also served at the Distinguished District 56 Governor for Toastmasters International. These professional positions as well as the volunteer positions have given me opportunities to achieve and to create Success.

What I discovered is that Success is not a destination, and it's not even about the journey. It has everything to do with what we do while on the journey. The lessons I learned while earning that mini-bike as a 12-year-old boy have certainly been more valuable than the bike itself. The magic working within me while I'm in the process of achieving is more valuable than the achievement itself.

Throughout this book, we will discuss the valuable lessons learned on my personal journey.

What is Success?

> *"Success is to be measured not so much by the position one has reached in life as by the obstacles he has overcame."*
>
> *Booker T. Washington*

Success is one of those abstract concepts that conjure up different meanings for each of us. It is like using the words "jiffy" or "a little bit" or "a smidgen." I am amazed that when I ask for a "couple" of some item, I am often asked if I want two or three. Even a "couple" has become somewhat obscure in meaning. I am curious. How would you define Success?

- Is your Success having more money? Or a mini-bike?

- Is it related to getting married?

- Is it having a different job or living in a different neighborhood?

- Is it about looking comfortable while delivering a speech or presentation?

- Might it be a restored relationship?

- Is it just about feeling better about yourself?

We've already established that Success is not about the journey, it is about what you do on the journey. Booker T. Washington clarified this further by saying it is about the obstacles that you overcome on the journey. When we have to use our power, strength, determination, and energy to overcome obstacles, we develop confidence that will Sustain Success. There are no shortcuts, and nothing creates confidence like overcoming. We stumble into a lot of things, but Sustainable Success is not one of them.

We can stumble into these obstacles, or we can prepare for them. Another lesson from my football days: I learned very quickly about momentum. If a defensive player and an offensive player are running toward each other to eventually collide, the one with the most momentum will be the one to deliver the blow. The one with the least momentum will be the one to receive the blow. The worst thing one can do is to slow down, because he will be on the receiving end of the impact.

When we do not spend time in preparation and we "stumble into obstacles," we receive the blow from those obstacles. It sets us back and causes us to stumble. When we prepare, we carry momentum through the obstacle, and this is where we create Sustainable Confidence and, ultimately, Sustainable Success.

In fact, Sustainable Success is created in preparation. The hardest part about preparation is just making the decision to get started.

Preparation

> *"It is not the will to win that matters, everyone has that. It is the will to prepare to win that matters."*
>
> *Paul "Bear" Bryant*

Preparation is the foundation for all Success; however, the battle is not in the preparation itself, it is in the will to prepare.

The Equation for Success:

*Success = **Preparation** + Opportunity*

What is the only portion of the equation that we control? ***Hint: It is in bold letters.*** We have no control over when and how the opportunities will present themselves. The only part of the equation we have any control over is PREPARATION! So, to what part of this equation should we apply our efforts? The answer is obvious!

In a formula, you have control over the inputs. This is not a formula because you only have control over one input. Please hold this equation near and dear to your heart.

Preparation is:

- A discipline, just as engineering, architecture, or medical practice; however, it is not Brain Surgery, Rocket Science, or even Magic.

- The process of creating <u>Personal Excellence</u>.

- A journey of becoming all you were created to be by waking up to the gifts and talents that are lying dormant deep within your soul.

Preparation is...the Bridge to Success.

Golden Nugget: Success rises and falls on preparation; nothing more, nothing less.

The quest for excellence demands preparation. Here is a thought: you and I are accomplishing things all the time. We take journeys every day. Therefore, we have daily opportunities to practice preparation.

Are you investing time in preparation?

- Do you enjoy what you are doing? If not, preparation could be the game changer.
- Are you overwhelmed? Do you have trouble keeping up with tasks? If so, the concepts of preparation in this book are for you.
- Is there something you would rather be doing? What is holding you back? Let's explore this question.
- Are you pursuing your dreams? If not, why not? Have bad experiences painted the wrong picture in your mind and set up false limitations and insecurities?
- If you enjoy what you are doing, you should have a passion for it. Do you have a passion for what you are spending your life on? If so, are you the best at your job that you can possibly be? You should be striving to be the best. _More often than not, the smallest adjustments have the greatest impact._ Small adjustments are implemented in preparation.
- Have you have ever had the following thought about your superiors: "I could do what he or she is doing and I could do it better, and yet I get paid half of their salary. Why not me? Why them? What's wrong with this picture?" Here is where many fall into the victim trap. Many make excuses rather than building a bridge to success. They believe that the success of others is luck and attributed to who they know. Companies do not

promote people. People promote themselves. Stay tuned, this concept could earn you a lot of money.

- Are you the "go to" guy or gal? Would you like to be? It is easier than your think.
- Is a fear of public speaking holding you back in your career? It does not have to. Preparation will make the difference. You can present like a pro. More to come.
- Do you shy away from conflict? No need to do so. Preparation is the key. You will learn how to prepare for the difficult conversations.

Success is not a destination, but a lifestyle or a discipline. Just as losing weight is a change in lifestyle, so is Success. Sit back and take a deep breath before reading the next quote by Aristotle. This gets me excited!

> "We are what we repeatedly do, therefore, Excellence is a Habit, not an act." Aristotle

Eureka! Listen to what Aristotle said. This one simple statement has the power to change your life. This is so simple but so profound. If you want to be excellent at something, then you must do it habitually, daily, or regularly. Remember, we are talking about Sustainable Success that stems from Sustainable Confidence.

Golden Nugget: The quest for Excellence is the fuel for Success. And this quest builds Sustainable Confidence.

Why this book about Success? The meaning of the word "Success" has become lost in meaningless gimmicks, fads, and clichés such as "fake it till you make it." Here is a little secret. Allowing ourselves to believe that we are going to "fake it until we make it" could end up adversely affecting our confidence. Our minds interpret this as "I am a fake." Faking it is an act and not a habit. This paints a picture in our minds that is not conducive to success, much less sustainable confidence.

I realize that my colleagues use the "fake it until we make it" cliché meaning that we should go ahead and take action and the feeling will come. For instance, if you don't feel like smiling, do it any way and the happy feeling will come. I get this and I agree with it. But at the same time, this concept has been misused. Trying to fake a sales presentation or a speech will fail every time. Trust me. I know firsthand. I contend that it is dangerous territory to go into something with "faking it" on our minds. Stay tuned...more to come on this matter. I have something really exciting to share about being a "Becomer" as opposed to being a "Faker."

For now, let's tackle another cliché that I'm sure you've heard, and one that inspired the title for this book: _"I'll cross that bridge when I get there."_ For grins, let's say you were on a toll road and approaching a toll both. You have to pay $1.75 for the toll, but you did not think about this until you reached the booth. Now you are holding up traffic looking for coins in your ashtray, your pocket, and on the floorboard. Look at the time wasted. What if you don't have $1.75? Not only were you inefficient, but you also lost valuable momentum. When we fail to plan we may or may not plan to fail, but we really do restrict our opportunities for Success. Success ONLY happens when preparation meets opportunity.

True Success depends on *Crossing That Bridge…BEFORE You Get There.* This book will focus on three principals for success: PREPARATION through PLANNING, PICTURING, and PURPOSE. These are not gimmicks, fads, or fiction and do not depend on faking it, but they do require practicing personal excellence.

This book will demonstrate how to awaken the gifts and talents that reside within you. Life is about crossing bridges. Every day we start journeys. Stumbling along these journeys does not create Sustainable Success. **Crossing That Bridge…BEFORE We Get There** through Preparation creates Sustainable Success.

I remember a very scary bridge that I crossed as a teenager, while living in Pearl, Mississippi. Since I grew up in Mississippi, most folks say that English is a second language for me. Fortunately, I moved to East Texas to learn English. (If you are from Texas you will get the humor. We joke about East Texas being backwards.)

Dad and I drove from Pearl to Tennessee to buy a camper cover for his truck. We left early in the morning and I drove part of the way. I remember driving on an old narrow road, and before I realized what was going on I found myself on a one-lane bridge—and I was fortunate that I did not meet oncoming traffic. I'll never forget the sudden panic I felt when I realized my predicament.

This was a physical bridge but is very symbolic of many predicaments in which we find ourselves. I have found myself in embarrassing situations because I did not invest proper time in preparation. Again, Success through preparation requires planning, picturing, and creating or finding purpose. Not investing time in preparation will cause failure and under-performance, and sometimes it can be outright dangerous, such as the time I thought I was Evil Knievel.

As a child, I always had a dirt bike around and spent many hours riding trails and jumping hills. Years later, when I was in my late twenties, I used to jog along Greens Bayou on the north side of Houston. As I jogged, I always admired the construction hill on the other side of the bayou and especially took note of the bike trail leading up the hill.

I dreamed of one day owning a bike again and jumping that construction hill. That day came! I purchased a used 1972 Yamaha 180 CC, Enduro. I, Evil Knievel Pitts, jumped on the bike full of testosterone and headed straight for the hill. It was a fairly tall hill, so I wound out second gear and hit that hill with enough torque and speed to send me airborne at the top. I launched myself over the top of the hill. It was while in flight that I had a FREEZE FRAME moment! I was reminded of the preparation I used to go through as a kid before going down a trail and certainly before jumping a hill.

This preparation involved slowly scoping out the trail or hill ahead of time. And this simple preparation was necessary to ensure that there were no surprises on the trail, the hill, and especially the other side of the hill. The typical surprise might resemble the one playing out before my very eyes. The hill had a very small landing area on top and certainly was not big enough for the velocity and trajectory of my flight. **I was airborne and flying over the top of the hill!** Furthermore, the trail took a 90-degree turn down the right side of the hill and on the backside was nothing but ruts and washouts. How I wish I would have **Crossed That Hill...BEFORE I Got There**. A little preparation would have made a big difference. Are you wondering what happened to me? You will find out shortly.

I can remember times when I gave public speeches or presentations and my message was lost in the distraction of my own nervousness. Has this ever happened to you? Does the thought of speaking before a crowd cause your jugulars to slap you in the face? One of the top three fears is public speaking, so if the very thought of it unnerves you, you are not alone. There is nothing more humiliating then falling apart in the middle of a presentation or speech. And there is nothing more rewarding than to hit a home run and to successfully share life-changing information with a group of people. So how would you like change lives, instead of falling apart?

The answer, again, is preparation. You might ask what preparation has to do with public speaking. The answer is **"Everything!"** If you will invest the energy into Preparation through Planning, Picturing, and Purpose, you will find success in public speaking. It is a simple matter of **Crossing That Bridge…BEFORE You Get There.**

The confidence gained by becoming an accomplished public speaker spills over to every area of your life. Some people walk barefoot on beds of hot coals to get the same results. I would rather pursue public speaking. Even if this is a tough area for you, you can also master public speaking. Let me say it a little louder with my virtual hands on your shoulders, "YOU CAN MASTER THE ART OF PUBLIC SPEAKING!" Do you want this? Stay with me.

Improper preparation has also caused me much pain at times in my career. One such example that comes to mind is the time when I received a large quote package on a low-margin product some years ago. We were given the target prices. My CEO lived in Ohio and would return to the company every other week. He agreed to meet with me on his next visit to discuss the margins on these products. I really thought that he would set up a meeting time and I could pull the data together. As it turned out, he came to my office and said he was ready. My heart sank. I had done nothing to prepare.

I pulled out the rather large folder of raw data and tried to make sense of it in his presence, and it was obvious that I was not prepared. If others do this to me, I call it "Vomiting Information." This was ugly and highly uncomfortable. I could feel the heat in my face as it turned bright red. It is not enough to have the intention to be prepared. I needed to have a stronger will to be prepared. There is the component of preparing early.

There is the component of summarizing to simplify for busy executives. Again, we are talking about **Crossing That Bridge…BEFORE You Get There**.

The story that I'm really fond of took place in Malaysia and is a story of **Crossing That Bridge…AFTER We Got There**. My sales engineer, Stan, was driving us from Singapore to Malaysia to visit a customer. As we crossed the bridge over the strait and cleared customs, we commented about the amount of traffic going into Singapore. A rather large number of Malaysians commute to Singapore daily for work, and they ride motorcycles. It is a sight to see. They usually ride double, they do not wear helmets, and they usually have sandals on their feet. They also ride in droves. We were glad we were entering Malaysia and not Singapore with the "millions" of motorbikes.

Stan took an exit after entering Malaysia…which actually turned out to be a U-turn, and guess what? You got it. We were now stuck in traffic entering Singapore—with those "millions" of bikes! It took about 45 minutes to clear customs. Stan was so frustrated that all he could say was, "I hate myself." Have you ever been so frustrated that you were at war with yourself? Stan and I continue laugh at this experience whereby he decided (by default) to cross that bridge after we got there.

Golden Nugget: If we do not make a conscious decision to "Cross That Bridge…BEFORE We Get There" we are making a default decision to "Cross that bridge after we get there."

If you haven't already figured it out, this book is about being a Bridge Crosser. The objective is to focus on Success through **Crossing That Bridge...Before You Get There.** The three specific principles that we will explore are PREPARATION by:

PLANNING

PICTURING

PURPOSE.

Golden Nuggets and Quotes:

- "Success is to be measured not so much by the position one has reached in life as by the obstacles he has overcame." Booker T. Washington

- "It is not the will to win that matters, everyone has that. It is the will to prepare to win that matters." Paul "Bear" Bryant

- Equation for Success:

  Success = **Preparation** + Opportunity

- Success rises and falls on preparation; nothing more, nothing less.

- "We are what we repeatedly do; therefore, Excellence is a Habit, not an act." Aristotle

- The quest for excellence is the fuel for success. And this quest builds Sustainable Confidence.

- Cross That Bridge ..Before You Get There through Preparation by Planning, Picturing, and Purpose.

- If we do not make a conscious decision to "Cross That Bridge...BEFORE We Get There" we are making a default decision to "Cross That bridge After We Get There."

Notes Page:

Reference	Page No.

Crossing That Bridge...BEFORE You Get There Demands

Planning

CHAPTER 2

PLANNING

> *"In my preparing for battle I have always found that plans are useless, but planning is indispensable."*
>
> *Dwight D. Eisenhower*

> *"Good plans shape good decisions. That's why good planning helps to make elusive dreams come true."*
>
> *Lester R. Bittel*

The difference between a plan and planning is that a plan could have been prepared by someone else, meaning you do not have any intellectual input. Planning implies that we have ownership and input with our very own creative genius.

Golden Nugget: Planning turns dreams into visions. It transforms ideas into goals. It puts feet to our desires. And it creates Sustainable Confidence, resulting in Sustainable Success.

Why did Eisenhower say that planning was indispensable? Planning brings out the best in us. Planning unleashes our creative genius. Planning gives discovery and growth to our gifts and talents. Planning allows us to encounter problems before we get to that bridge.

In 1962, John F. Kennedy gave a speech at Rice Stadium. In this historic oration, he announced that Americans were going to the moon. He specifically said, *"We choose to go to the moon. We choose to go to the moon this decade and to do other things, not because they are easy, but because they are hard, **because that goal will serve to organize and measure the best of our energies and skills**."*

This message was about creating a BIG goal, reaching for the moon, and then immersing ourselves in preparation through planning, painting a picture of what success looks like, and bathing it in purpose.

Allow me to paraphrase his words...and maybe take some literary license: *"When we reach for our personal moon or stretch ourselves with a BIG goal, this goal organizes (calls to action our talents) and measures (dispenses talent in proportion to the largeness of the task) the best of our skills and energies (it awakens and deploys those gifts and talents lying dormant in each of us)."*

Golden Nugget: If you do not intend to mow, then do you need a lawnmower? If Michael Jackson never endeavored to sing or dance, that raw and pure talent would have existed only in seed form.

Reaching for the moon is not achieved merely through desire to reach the goal, but through planning. A desire is a mere dream. Planning makes it a goal. "Organizing and measuring the best of our skills and energies" refers to planning. Here is a great revelation: Reaching for our personal moon is done in the planning stages, and this is where **Personal Excellence** is achieved.

The entire space mission was carried out on paper before it was ever deployed. **Crossing that Bridge BEFORE They Got There** seemed like a small step for Neil Armstrong, but it was a giant leap toward the success of the project. This was an example of an organization setting lofty goals and supporting those goals with the pillars of planning. Not only can organizations find success through planning, so can we as individuals.

On January 5, 2009, US Air Flight 1549 took off from LaGuardia and struck a flock of Canadian Geese. The jet ultimately lost engine power. What was amazing was the calm, reassuring attitude of Captain Chelsey B. "Sully" Sullenberger as he announced that he was going to make an emergency landing on the Hudson River. He announced this as if it were routine. Actually, for Sully, it was routine. Sully had prior experience as a glider pilot in the Air Force. Even more amazing than this heroic feat is what he told reporters after the fact. He said that he often strategized as to what he would do if he encountered engine failure upon take off. **He Crossed That Bridge...BEFORE He Got There.** He planned and strategized. Not only did he save the lives of 150 passengers, but also large numbers of lives in the heavily populated New York City. I mentioned earlier that not **Crossing That Bridge...BEFORE You Get There** could also be dangerous—but with a little planning, you can avoid those obstacles.

Let's return to the moment I found myself airborne on that

Yamaha flying over the top of a hill. I had no experience as a glider pilot, nor did I have a plan. I landed on the backside of the hill and successfully navigated the ruts and washouts. It could have been luck that kept me from wiping out, but I believe there was a purpose for keeping me around. I had a book that I was supposed to write and lives that I was supposed to change. I needed a story for my book. I got by with that one, but being around bikes all my life, I know many that have lost their lives performing less stupid stunts than mine. We do not have to depend on being lucky. We can make our journey one of planning and our destiny one of Success.

Golden Nugget: *We do not have to depend on being lucky. We can make our journey one of planning and our destiny one of Success.*

It is a common perception that people who write down goals are far more successful. They are much more likely to achieve their goals than those who merely think about their goals.

Years ago, the company for which I worked asked us to come up with goals for the New Year. We shared our goals and never talked about them again. Three years later, I found the goals on a piece of paper in my desk drawer and realized that I had accomplished them all. This is not an ideal way to treat goals. For goals to have the most impact, they should have benchmarks and status updates. My point here is that even just writing a goal down puts you on a path for completion. However, if things are important they get measured. Goals need to be supported by the pillars of planning. Planning allows us to make regular installments to our goals and dreams. As we invest, we slowly become the person who carries dreams and the success thereof.

What activities should we aim our planning toward? The three areas of planning that have impacted my life the most are: my **Values**, my **Daily Task Journal**, and **Communication**, which includes presentations, speeches, and one-on-one.

My Values

We need to know what we stand for before we are tempted. Having a set of core values can make us successful and can even make us a hero.

I am reminded of the plane that crashed into the 14th Street Bridge over the Potomac River on January 13, 1982. The plane carried 74 passengers and 5 crew members, and took 7 cars with it into the freezing river. There were 6 survivors from the plane crash. Arland Williams was one of those survivors…at least initially. He stayed behind to pass lifelines to the other passengers, and after passing the lifeline to the last passenger he slipped away under the water a hero. The last passenger that he passed the life line to was unable to hang on due to the hypothermia numbing her body. Lenny Skutnik was standing on the shore receiving the passengers and helping them to dry land. He dove into the freezing water to rescue the woman who had lost the ability to hold to the lifeline and was disappearing under the water. Both men had values that made them willing to give their lives for a fellow human being. Both were willing, one had the ultimate call.

While you and I may never be called to sacrifice our life for another, we can have the same courage and commitment to our values **By Crossing That Bridge…BEFORE We Get There.** We can stand strong in the hour of temptation and not take the easy way out.

How would you react to the following scenarios?

- A person of the opposite sex says that he or she wants to talk to you and asks if you could meet for lunch. On the surface, this does not seem bad, but it could give the appearance of evil. Suppose a friend of your spouse sees you with this other person?

- A salesperson offers you a large sum of money to divert business his or her way.

- Everyone at work has turned against a coworker with allegations that you know are not true. To tell the truth will cause you to possibly be the next victim.

- Someone at work is being treated with hostility. Are you willing to stand up for a fellow human?

- You are invited to go to a gentlemen's club. Or customers demand that you take them to a gentlemen's club and entertain them on the company card. How would you handle this?

Our value system is our navigator and it will give us light and wisdom in planning and deployment. How did you answer these questions? Did you feel somewhat unprepared for any of these? Perhaps you have had a personal experience with one of these scenarios. Our answers should give us some insight into where we need to shore up our values.

We cannot do anything about the past, but the future provides us the opportunity to prepare and work on subpar values. How do we improve our less than stellar values? I recommend writing down those key values, committing them to memory, and reciting them daily. If we do this, we will stand strong against the storms of temptation.

Golden Nugget: Our values are an anchor amidst the storms of temptation.

Have you ever grown your own vegetable garden? The one thing that I hate about a vegetable garden is that you have to weed it regularly.

I have learned that weeds grow much faster than vegetables. In addition, they do not produce fruit. They produce a whole bunch of seed that in turn grow fast and produce a more seed. Negative things seem to move at a whole lot faster pace than positive things—and that includes values.

Weeding a garden can be hard work but has great rewards. If a vegetable garden is not weeded, the weeds will overtake the vegetables. They will rob the vegetables of their water and nutrients and ultimately choke them out. On the other hand, pulling the weeds out by the roots and throwing them into the fire promotes healthy vegetables. If we pull the weeds when they are young and tender, they are easily removed. If we allow them to grow big and strong and take root, they are hard to remove.

Have you been tempted about something as simple as telling a white lie to make a problem go away? This represents the critical crossroad. We have two choices. We can pull these weeds when they are young and tender thoughts. Or we can allow them to grow big and strong and to take root. These weeds will overtake our minds and rob them of nutrients. Weeding out the bad values and thoughts will certainly strengthen our values and keep us from indiscretions.

I am reminded of the pine trees that I used to shimmy up as a kid. It took a lot of work to climb up the tree. These were the tall pines without any limbs except for at the very the top. It would take a long time and a lot of energy to climb up the tree. Coming down was a controlled slide and highly dangerous. If you ever relaxed your grip too much, it would be a freefall all the way to the bottom. If we do not have a firm grip on our values, it can be a freefall to the bottom.

Golden Nugget: We would never compromise our values if we lived up to the character that our dogs think we have.

Consider, for instance, how fast Lance Armstrong has fallen from grace. How about Tiger Woods? What about Joe Paterno? He had a great career as Head Football Coach at Penn State University from 1968 to 2011. Do you recall how quickly this legend's success unraveled? It can be hero to zero in a moment of time.

The positive things you do at work, as well as in public or private life, will slowly and steadily grow a firm foundation. This foundation will support you in every endeavor. It takes years of positive daily installments to build that success, while one indiscretion can unravel those successes at lightning speed. It is never too late to start making installments.

Have you ever walked up a slippery creek bank? I have and I can remember taking small but sure steps up the bank to keep from slipping. But the minute I slip, I slide all the way back to the bottom. Once the slide has started, there is nothing we can do but endure the ride down. Our value system provides us with those slow but sure steps to prevent a massive backslide. We simply cannot wait until we are in the middle of a crisis or temptation to determine what we are made of or what we will do. If we want to live successful lives, **Crossing That Bridge…BEFORE We Get There** is a must as it relates to our values.

We can ill afford a misstep. If we have an indiscretion and someone discovers it, the results can be devastating. Just ask Lance. Here is a major eye-opener: Even if we are not caught in a dishonest or negative act, it can still severely hinder our success.

Golden Nugget: A guilty conscience is a cancer that erodes the very foundation of our confidence.

Friends, here is where the rubber meets the road. You have heard it said that we can do anything we set our minds to. Let's first of all agree that "anything" is really "anything within a reasonable range of our gifts and talents." For instance, I could not be a professional lineman in the NFL nor could I be a singer, professional or otherwise. If you don't believe me about the singing, you can ask Karen Denise, my wife. She is the one who turns the radio up louder when I try to make joyful noise. I actually think I sing wonderfully…I just tear it up something awful getting it out.

Regarding the cliché "we can do anything we set our minds to"—I wish to revise it. It should actually be "we can do anything we set our guilt-free minds to." A guilty conscience is like a cancer that erodes our very confidence.

Golden Nugget: We can do anything we set our guilt-free minds to.

Any time we violate our own values, we have guilt. Guilt has a voice, and it talks to us. In order to reach for our Personal Excellence, we have to stretch ourselves, and part of confidence is feeling good about who we are. When we endeavor to become more than we are and what we were created to be, we need confidence motivating us with positive messages. If there is guilt, we have an adversarial message...a message that weighs us down and consumes our thoughts as we attempt to climb the ladder to our Personal Excellence. Guilt fertilizes the weeds in our minds. Confidence is the fruit of a pure conscience.

By the way, did you know that worry can clutter your conscience as well? It can be an even larger drag on your energy and creative genius. It can devastate your confidence. There is more to come on worry...

Golden Nugget: Guilt and worry fertilize the weeds in our minds. A pure conscience is the foundation of a confidence. And confidence is the fruit of a pure conscience.

I want to briefly talk about one last issue. It is about holding unforgiveness or holding a grudge. I have heard Joe McGee say time and time again that holding unforgiveness is like eating rat poison...and waiting for the rat to die.

> *Holding unforgiveness is like eating rat poison... and waiting for the rat to die.*   *Joe McGee*

In addition to the rat poison causing you to have ill health and eventually killing you, unforgiveness will also destroy your creative genius. It will keep you from having a clear conscience. It will consume energy that could have been better allocated for productive things. We must know for what we stand.

Being that person of character does not happen automatically. In fact, our minds are being programmed every minute of every day by default. What do I mean by "programming"? I mean that we are passively receiving information all the time.

Think about the farmers of our grandparents' era. They worked from sun up until sundown, usually behind a mule and a plow. There was nothing influencing their minds but their own introspection. Today, we have an onslaught of information bombarding our minds every minute of every day. We have billboards, TV, the internet, and newspapers telling us what we are or should be thinking about. We have subtle thoughts such as, "Should I tell a white lie to make this problem go away?"

If we do not counter the influx of passive programming with intentional programming, we lose this war. I was driving on

Interstate 45 at a high speed when a piece of debris landed in my lane. I felt a jolt of electricity through my left arm commanding it to jerk the wheel hard left and NOW!. At the same time, my experience overrode that message and kept me in my lane as I did not have time to confirm that there was no other vehicles to my left. That overriding-experience is like a ground rod that diffuses the electrical impulses. This is a classic example of an involuntary impulse being overridden by a voluntary action...an action breathed in to existence over many years of experience. The influx of information hitting our brains daily appeals to our involuntary or natural responses. Planning allows us to override with a voluntary response. I like to remind myself of the person I have chosen to be. I like to tell myself:

- I am a man of integrity. I will avoid even what could appear to be an indiscretion. If there is an expense that is questionable, I will pay it and not charge it to the company. I will tell the truth. (With this decision to tell the truth, it makes it difficult to do something that will later make me feel compelled to lie.) I will be true to my wife. I will be a faithful employee.

- I am a kind man. I will treat people with respect and kindness. I will follow Stephen Covey and seek to understand before seeking to be understood. I will walk in the light of John Maxwell's truth that people don't care how much you know until they know how much you care.

- I am a thankful man. I am thankful for my blessings and all that I have. I will remember the man who complained about not having shoes until he met the man who did not have any feet.

- I will give back. I will help others to be all they have been created to be. I will use my means to help the less fortunate. I will follow the advice of the late great Zig Ziglar. He said that if we help enough people get what they want out of life, we will have everything we want.

- I am a reliable man. I will produce results for the company for which I work. I will be true to my word.

- I will walk in forgiveness. I will not eat rat poison. I choose to follow Bobby McFerrin's lyrics "Don't worry, be happy." (I know. The tune is now stuck in my head too.)

Without a good value system governing our lives, we are on the threshold of a backslide. Planning is where we achieve Personal Excellence even when it comes to our values. Personal Excellence is also achieved in planning our Daily Tasks.

Daily Tasks

Earlier, we discussed written goals and how writing them on paper increases the chances of completion. Daily Tasks are nothing more than goals. A goal is a goal is a goal.... Daily tasks (goals) need just as much planning as long-term goals. We need a way to capture and manage tasks.

If you desire more output and better efficiencies, then **Cross Those TASKS…BEFORE You Get There**…unless you are in love with the Easter Egg Hunt. I have used journals for task management for many years. I have also used more sophisticated Excel spreadsheets. Spreadsheets are great if you are tied to a desk, but if you need mobility, they offer challenges. I find that a journal works best for mobility. I also find that I have a more intimate relationship with my pen and paper. That is, what I physically write I remember better.

What has the daily Task Journal done for me?

1. The Task Journal has substantially increased my **Output**.

2. The Task Journal has created **Time Savings**. It has allowed me to avoid the Easter Egg Hunt. Charlie! What's the Easter Egg Hunt? Be patient, Grasshopper. Almost there....

3. The Task Journal has provided an avenue for **Downloading**. It allows me quick downloading of ideas and thoughts before I forget them. I just hate it when I have an idea that will make me a millionaire and later I can't recall the idea. There is nothing left but the flavor.

4. The Task Journal has provided a place for me to **Consolidate** information. I use my journal to take notes, as well, and therefore I have one spot for all important information.

Output

I have significantly increased my daily output by journaling. I am not working more hours but am simply capitalizing on time saved by the efficiencies gained through Task Journaling. If a task is not completed today, it rolls over. For the purpose of clarity, from this point on when I use the words "Task Journaling," I mean capturing and managing tasks.

There are tasks that get rolled over for a long time...but they stay in the front and center until they are complete. I am reminded daily that a task still needs to be done. As we put off tasks waiting on the time to work on them, we tend to forget them. Herein is the real power of the Task Journal. The tasks are managed from inception to completion.

There are times when you may have a small window of opportunity that is ideal for hitting those small, non-urgent tasks. For instance, you may have meetings scheduled all day and half-hour breaks in between. There is not enough time to really delve into your most pressing tasks. Having the tasks written allows you take a quick look and pick those tasks small enough to fit this window of opportunity. It may be making a phone call or sending an email. It may be looking up information. And by the way, many smaller tasks are usually out of mind. Without these written down, I would have to depend on happenstance—they are not easily retrievable when my mind is already so filled with to-dos. Written, they are always at my fingertips. **The end result of journaling tasks is productivity!**

Now, let me share with you how to leverage your Task Journal. You can really capitalize by capturing these small non-urgent tasks as they manifest. This includes capturing appropriate information from emails, voicemails, and those items that happen to pop up in your mind. By capturing these tasks, not only do you increase **productivity**, you will be able to save time. The Easter Egg Hunt should only be on Easter. Capturing tasks and information creates huge time savings.

Time Savings

My Gosh! The massive amount of emails and voicemails I receive daily are so challenging. I receive so many important emails that are not necessarily urgent, and I end up having to put them off until later. When later arrives I have received so many more emails that the one I am looking for is buried. Then I can't remember the name of the person who sent it. I can't remember the date it was received. Then I spend the next 20 to 30 minutes on the Easter Egg Hunt. Have you figured out what the Easter Egg Hunt is? Have you ever had someone send you an email from an address they have never used before? Perhaps your email program decides to list the name in a different order. Wasting valuable time searching for that one item, hidden among many, is the Easter Egg Hunt.

When it's really bad, I'll spend so much time looking and searching that I forget what I am looking for. Stop laughing! I would bet you have done the same thing. I do this much less these days because I work my Task Journal.

Then there are voicemails. Do you use your messaging feature to stage work? I do...then I forget who left the important message and have to listen to 30 messages to find the one that I just vaguely remember. You can dynamically capture this in the Task Journal and avoid the Easter Egg Hunt.

Emails and voicemails that get thrown into the "I will address this one later" bucket get special treatment in my Task Journal as I capture the critical information. If it requires an action from me, I create an entry in my journal. If it is an email, the important information that I capture is the name as it appears on the email and the date it was received.

If it is a voicemail, I capture the name of the person, the subject matter, and a call-back number. This allows me to quickly make a call, when I only have a small window of time, without the Easter Egg Hunt.

Not only do I capture emails and voicemails, I can gain even more leverage in my journal by capturing the voices in my head! We all have these voices. My voices are always saying, "Don't forget to do this or that, remember this and remember that. Charlie, you are so good looking!" Well, maybe not the latter. When these voices are spitting out important things I need to remember, I am able to download them to the Task Journal.

Downloading

Have you ever had a great idea and a few hours later, you were left with the most succulent flavor but no substance? You don't remember what the thought was. This is like having a phenomenal dream, waking up with the full emotions of the dream, and yet not being able to remember it.

Have you had someone remind you of a task and you immediately say, "Why just this morning, I was thinking about how I need to get that done." The sad reality is you have probably had this déjà vu regarding this same task several times.

Using a task list allows you to quickly download so that the task cannot be forgotten. If I am driving, I make notes on the recorder app on my iPhone. Then before the day is up, I download those notes to my Task Journal. This too allows me to capture and put the task front and center and provides great opportunities to bring it to completion. Not only am I capturing important information, I also use my Task Journal as a depot to consolidate important information.

Consolidation of Information

Over the years, I have grabbed a "Big Chief" tablet...oops, I wonder how many of my readers know what this is? Let me start over. In the past, I have grabbed an 8-1/2 x 11 tablet to take meeting notes. I would ultimately accumulate a half dozen of these. Then when I needed to refer back to my notes, again, I would spend time on the Easter Egg Hunt trying to find the meeting notes. Now all of my meeting notes go right into my journal, and I have one spot where I consolidate all of my notes. In addition, every entry is dated. The other added benefit is that the journal and notes are in chronological order.

Look, we as citizens of this fast-paced, highly technical new world order are required to accomplish so much more than the previous generations were. There is no way for our minds to manage the long list of ever-changing tasks that are required of us. The overload causes stress and sometimes memory loss as well. We need quick access to our tasks and do not need to waste time on the Easter Egg Hunt. Avoiding the Easter Egg Hunt is analogous to removing the bottlenecks in LEAN manufacturing. Have you read *The Goal* by Eliyahu Goldratt? I highly recommend the book.

The heart of this book is centered around a plant manager,

Alex Rogo, and the ultimatum given to him to turn the plant around in three months. It was only when Alex's job was in jeopardy that he consulted a previous coworker, Jonah the physicist. One of the questions that Jonah asked him was, "What is the goal of the business?" The answer was to make money, so the two of them set out to remove the bottlenecks. Removing bottlenecks in a manufacturing facility increases efficiencies, resulting in greater profits. Removing bottlenecks in our day-to-day routines increases our efficiencies and results in greater profits for the company as well. It also increases your value.

Try journaling your tasks…remember, Personal Excellence is created in planning. I have used a definite program for journaling my tasks for years, and I have formalized my method over the past year.

On the next page is a sample of the format that I designed for my Task Journal. At the top of the page, I have a place for the day, date, and starting as well as ending mileage.

The first section is for my appointments for the day. The second section is labeled "Primary Tasks for Today" and is for listing my priority tasks for the day. I have a field for a deadline and a field for comments. If this task is related to an email that has more relevant information, I will add a reference about the email in the comment section. I also include the sender's name and a date. If I had an email from Joe Blow, it would be written in this formant, "em J. Blow, 1/7/13." This allows me to quickly find that email again and with no Easter Egg Hunt.

The last section, labeled "Task Capture Log," is where I capture action items from emails, voice messages, and ideas. These emails, voice messages, and ideas eventually move up to the task list. Or, they may be completed without being moved up because I have a small window of opportunity to complete them. In the sample below, I have deleted rows to make the form fit this page.

Task Journal Format:

Day		Date	
Starting Mileage		Ending Mileage	
Appointments			
Time	Appointment	Ref	Location/Comment
Primary Task for Today			
No.	Task	Deadline	Comments
Task Capture Log			
No.	Task	Source	Comments

My Tasks Journal comprises the page shown above and on the backside is a notes page. When I open my journal, I have the task page on the right side of the binding and the notes page on the left side of the binding. If I have notes relevant to a task, I put them in the notes page and reference them in the comment field of the respective task in the journal. If I take notes during a meeting, I put them in the notes section of my journal.

Using a Task Journal allows us to manage our tasks instead of our tasks managing us and launching us into the Easter Egg Hunt. It puts us in the driver's seat of our own destiny. If managing and planning tasks are important to enhancing our chances for success, how much more does the concept of planning pertain to communication? Let's explore the concept.

Communication

Communication is the one area that can create the greatest contrast between you and your colleagues and coworkers in regards to success. Success demands that we master the art of communication. We cannot always help what is heard, but we can plan for it, set the tone, anticipate it, and ask questions for feedback to ensure understanding.

Golden Nugget: Mastering the art of communication is the fastest bridge to promotion and more pay.

Dale Carnegie shared in his book, *How to Win Friends and Influence People*, that the highest paid engineers he knows are not the smartest and most talented engineers. The highest paid were the engineers who were good communicators. The engineers who make the big bucks are those who can articulate an idea and sell management on its value, who can create a team and sell them on the vision, and who can articulate the value of the project to investors.

So what does planning have to do with communication? It has everything to do with it. I am sure you have tried to communicate something, but what you said was not what was heard and the whole conversation spiraled out of control. Maybe folks were offended over what they heard, which you and I know very well is not what we said. Have you ever tried to share something and had to start over several times because the receiver was just not following you?

> The single biggest problem in communication is the illusion that it has taken place.   George Bernard Shaw

Spending many years in supervision and management, I discovered that I was thought of as a "Big Dog" by plant workers and that my voice carried authority. I can remember walking out to the plant with the goal of finding out the status of a part. I would ask one of the production workers if they could tell me the status. The next thing I know, I am being called into the GM's office and taken to task for changing priorities.

I simply asked about status. What the worker heard was, "This order is hot. Stop everything you are doing and jump on it." I learned to set the tone of the conversation by stating my objective for asking the question. "First of all, I am not asking for you to change anything you are doing. I know you have priorities and do not want you to change those. I am simply trying to find out the status of a part." This approach made all the difference in the world—it was perfectly clear communication.

Other times I would go out to ask a similar question of the shipping supervisor, and she would immediately start yelling at me that she couldn't just stop what she was doing and jump on something just because I thought it was hot. With this individual, I would state the objective of my question but I would also make sure she was listening by asking her if she understood that I was not changing priorities but simply looking for information.

The other thing I learned is that when there was a problem in the plant, and I walked out and asked what happened, the workers heard my statement as an accusation that someone had made a mistake or caused the problem. I learned to say, "I am not interested in fixing blame, I just want to understand what happened and what you think we need to do to fix it so that it does not happen again." Remember that as a supervisor, your voice carries authority and accusation. This is true even if the person to whom you are speaking is not a direct report.

If we want positive results, we have to accept responsibility for what is said as well what is heard. This is an art. This is what separates leaders from managers.

> "The art of communication is the language of leadership."
> James Humes

A personal and funny example of communication not taking place is with my son Josh. This story revolves around my jogging excursions along Greens Bayou and Josh's desire to go with me. He was three years old and he always asked to go jogging with me. I would typically take my older son, Jason. He rode his bike alongside, but the picture on the return journey looked very different, with Jason on my shoulders and his bike in my hand. Wow! It ended up being a great workout.

Josh always asked to go. There was no way I could take him with me because he could not keep up, I'd not be able to keep an eye on him, and therefore I would not get a workout myself. My answer was always the same: "Josh, I can't take you because you won't be able to keep up." I had a bright idea one day. I could take him to the track and keep an eye on him as I jogged circularly. So I announced to him that the next time I went jogging, I would do it at the track and he could join me.

Nothing could have prepared me for his response. He had a look on his face like, "I am not that stupid." He said, "Daddy, if I can't keep up at the creek, I can't keep up at the track." That was actually brilliant logic. He was right. I thought I was communicating that I could watch him at the track, but what he heard was in reference to keeping up. Our understanding was on different levels, as is our daily communication. Even if we are on the same level as a person intellectually, we may be in different places emotionally. This changes by the minute.

The point here is that it is our responsibility as leaders to meet people at their level. If we are the communicator, we must plan an approach that fits our audience. If we are the listener, we must make sure we seek to understand. Communication is the skill that separates leaders from managers. It is the difference between being and being an achiever or just an employee

Another example happened with my wife. I have some hearing loss, and therefore mine and Karen's conversations can get interesting and entertaining. Hearing loss keeps a marriage fun. She had been on call for several Sundays in a row. As we approached this particular Sunday, she said, "I am going to make it to Church this Sunday for my careless abominations." I knew that she was not going to church because of "careless abominations." Because I am used to having to connect the dots, I figured out that she actually said, "I am going to church this Sunday if it (harelips a nation)" not "for my careless abominations."

Another evening, we were eating some homemade chicken tortilla soup. She really outdid herself this time on the soup. As I sat on the recliner and my soup cooled on the TV tray, she walked by and asked me, "What time is it?" I replied that it was 6:30. Judging by the look on her face I realized that I had answered a question that she did not ask. I quickly thought about what sounds like "What time is it?" I came up with the only other question she could have been asking me in light of the fact we were eating chicken tortilla soup. I stated, "I think you actually asked, 'How is it?'" I received a one word answer: "Yes."

Whether you have hearing loss or not, we can hear incorrectly and, many times, understand incorrectly. As leaders and communicators, we need to plan for this.

Golden Nugget: Great communication starts with great planning.

Have you ever tried to talk to your boss about something and his interpretation of what you were trying to communicate or even your motives takes the conversation into a different direction? Or he simply could not understand what you were trying to say. Have you ever felt like you have lost total control of a conversation and did not know how to bring it back? What about trying to ask a direct report to do a task differently and the only thing they hear is, "He said I am doing a bad job."

What about needing to have a very tough or sensitive conversation and you are struggling with how to structure the approach?

Whether the communication is to be written or it is to be verbal, always start with the question:

"What outcome do I want to achieve with my communication?"

Don't ever start a journey if you do not know your destination. We cannot create a road map or a plan if we do not know where we are going. In addition to telling us what outcome we desire, the answer to this question also tells us what our motive is and allows us to explore what approach may be best for the desired outcome.

Secondly, write your communication down and read it to see if it supports your desired outcome. Role play and pretend you are the recipient of the message. Ask yourself how you would feel if it was your boss delivering this message to you.

Always set the tone of the conversation right from the beginning. If is a tough or sensitive conversation, it is best to process your opening. You may want to have some greetings and maybe there are other subjects of a lighter note that can be discussed first. You may consider stating your objectives for the conversation or even have a written agenda. The most important part of any communication is the opening and how we process it. This is not only important with one-on-one conversations—it is important for speeches and presentations, as well.

Speeches and Presentations

In a speech or presentation, the opening is where we grab the attention of our audience and introduce our theme. In one-one-one conversations, the opening is where we set the tone and expectations of the communication. Writing it down and reading it allows us to encounter the best strategy before delivery. Again, we create Personal Excellence when we plan, which allows us **to Cross That Bridge BEFORE We Get There.**

Do you give speeches or presentations? Start with the two questions:

1. What outcome do I want to achieve with my communication?

2. If I were able to boil my speech down to one sentence, what would it be?

These questions flush out our motivation and our theme. The two most important parts of a speech or a presentation are the opening and closing. I encourage you to memorize these two but do not try to memorize the entire speech. People will remember mostly the first and last items you say and very little in the middle. We have one chance to give a good first impression and to get their attention with the opening. We have one final opportunity to drive it home in the conclusion.

Writing out a speech or presentation and reading over it allows you to plan transitions, create flow, and discover opportunities for illustrative stories and humor. It allows you to encounter possible objections and to deal with them way in advance. It allows us to **Cross That Bridge...BEFORE We Get There.**

One-on-One Communication

Communication is a process, and therefore planning the process for maximum impact is a must. The more delicate the situation, the more important the planning becomes. Use the OLD method.

O – Outcome. Ask the question, "What outcome do I desire?"

L – Locate your audience. What is their mindset? Are they upset? Are they closed minded or are they open minded? You may have to play verbal tennis and ask questions to determine the mindset of your audience. Is there a management/blue collar gap? Is there an age or education gap?

D - Design a bridge to move the audience from current position to desired outcome.

Are you faced with a tough conversation? Do you have to correct an employee? Are you giving a speech about an unpopular and possibly a volatile subject?

When having to have a tough conversation with a direct report to get them back on track, I like to validate their value right from the beginning. I want to set the tone from the start. For instance, if Carla was being short with coworkers and I needed to address it, I would first ask, **"What outcome do I want for my communication?"**

Do I want to tell her off and feel big and powerful? (By the way, rudeness is a weak man's strength.)

> "Rudeness is a weak man's strength." Eric Hoffer

Do I want to humiliate her and take the chance of her walking out? Do I want her to perform poorly in areas where she is currently performing well because she was hurt by my communication? No, what I really want is for her to make a simple adjustment. For instance, if I needed get Carla to make an adjustment in how she deals with her coworkers, it might go something like this:

"Carla, first of all, you are not in trouble. In fact, I want to say that you are a key employee and I want to thank you for the

value you bring to the company. And what I mean by that is you have great intellect. You can hear about a problem, go through the list of possible causes in your head, and have a solution before most of us can even figure out where to start. In addition, you are a master at task management and you have the ability to switch to people-mode when a customer calls. This is a rare trait. **What I want to talk to you about today is an adjustment that I think will make you even more effective.** *You do great with managing tasks and handling customers. It is my observation, though, that you tend to treat your coworkers as tasks, and it comes across as you are angry or perturbed with them. I'll bet you did not even know that you were coming across that way. Carla, would you agree with this assessment?"*

First of all, I made sure that I relieved Carla of her number one fear. Any time we get called to the boss' office, our first thought is, "What have I done now?" If I would have just started talking, she would only hear that she is doing a bad job.

I affirmed Carla for what she does well. I start with affirmation and make my transition by stating that there is an adjustment that will make her even more effective. In a way, I have also given her a reputation to live up to. I want her to meet the standard she set. In this conversation, giving her a reputation to live up to is subtle, but we can also hit this area more aggressively if necessary. I have yet to say that she is doing a bad job. I state my observation and then ask if she agrees with this assessment. By asking Carla if she agrees with this assessment, I am **locating my audience.**

I am creating a dialogue as opposed to a monologue or a lecture. I am engaging her help in solving the problem. I will use Carla's answer to begin designing a bridge to get us to the desired adjustment. I can get more out of Carla by focusing on the things she does well and encouraging her to bring some under-par areas up to the standard she has set. And last but not least, I am engaging her to help with the solution. In this way, you can discipline an employee and have them thank you for it. It is absolutely amazing the impact good planning can have.

Whenever we start criticizing someone, their defenses go up. This is natural. Here is the secret to understanding this phenomenon; criticism always shouts to the person being criticized, "Your intentions are bad." The inner thoughts of those being criticized fights back with, "My intentions are good and I did not intend for those results. All the great things I do for the company and I don't get a thank you. All I get is a chewing when something does not go right. Do they not realize all the things I do right and all the money I make for this company?"

Always give the person the benefit of the doubt for having good intentions. This is exactly what I did in my opening to Carla. In this example, I validated Carla's value and gave her the benefit of the doubt for having good intentions. It is easy for us to criticize and easy for others think we are judging their intentions. Why? Because we do not give others the same benefit of the doubt that we give ourselves. You and I never have bad intentions. But yet, we are quick to suggest that others do by our actions. When we criticize, we are attacking intentions. There is no excuse for not realizing that our actions are having this impact on others. If we want to **Cross That Bridge...BEFORE We Get There**, we must take responsibility for creating effective communication. Take a look at what John Maxwell said.

> "We judge ourselves by our intentions but we judge others by what they do."   John Maxwell

We should always give others the same benefit of the doubt that we extend to ourselves. If we practiced this one concept in our communication, it would transform our effectiveness. My Dad found this to be a useful tool when I was a teen.

As a teen, my relationship with my Dad was strained and somewhat awkward. This all began to change as he began to validate my worth. He did not use wordy approbations but very simple statements to communicate my value to him. He would ask me questions and really seem to like my answers. He would praise my thought process. He would start sentences off with a simple statement such as, "Well, you and I are alike in that..." or "You and I understand these things." His simple statements communicated that we had something in common and that this was a good thing. It showed his approval of me. The acceptance of my Dad did wonders for my confidence and our relationship. Everyone needs validation. Thanks, Dad.

An example of how I used the OLD approach happened in 2008. The company for which I worked was being acquired by another entity. We had a record year and raises were due to our employees. The problem was that we had signed the letter of intent and we could not alter our financial status. After the acquisition was launched and the due diligence began, the collapse of the banking industry followed. Therefore it took considerably longer than anticipated for closing.

My GM and I went to the corporate office to speak with the CEO of the company that was acquiring us. We needed to state our case for giving the long overdue raises. This required a definite game plan.

The desired outcome was obvious; we needed to reward the hard work of our team and we needed the CEO to agree to allow it.

As far as locating my audience, this was a bit more difficult. My only exposure to the CEO was related to the acquisition. Nevertheless, he was an upbeat, positive, and motivational leader. I pegged him as one who would appreciate the value of the team. Most successful business leaders have read the book *Good to Great* by Jim Collins.

I used this book as my bridge and the lead-in to make my point. In this book, the studies and research proved that the difference between good companies and great companies is the people. As I began sharing that our employees are our assets and that is what made our company great, I asked if he ever read the book *Good to Great*. He shared with me that he actually worked for Danaher, which was featured in *Good to Great*. Wow! I could not have designed a better bridge. He knows exactly from whence I was coming.

As it turned out, we were able to move forward with the raises. The point here is that I made every effort to **Cross That Bridge Ahead of Time** through planning. Could my plan have been better? Certainly! There is always room for improvement. But a mediocre plan is better than no plan at all.

In one-on-one conversations, use the OLD approach we've explored in this section. Start by defining the desired Outcome. Then, Locate your audience. And finally, Design a bridge connecting the minds set of your audience to the desired destination. The more planning you do ahead of time, the more effective you will be.

Preparation is where we create Personal Excellence. It is not the will to win...but the will to PREPARE to win that creates success. If success is defined as Preparation + Opportunity, then the only part of the equation we control is the PREPARATION part.

Prepared Speeches & Presentations

Investing the proper amount of energy and preparation into our speeches and presentations will pay tremendous dividends. There are three basic components to a speech or a presentation: Opening, Body, and Conclusion. These three have a symbiotic relationship, meaning that they feed off of each other. One does not exist without the other. It is like a ham and cheese sandwich. It takes bread, ham, and cheese to have that type of sandwich. If you are missing one item, you do not have a H&C sandwich.

The Opening – Grab their Attention

The most important objectives for an opening are to grab the attention of the audience and to introduce the theme. When we are introduced to an audience, we must remember that their minds are all over the place.

Before you even begin speaking, you should utilize the person introducing you. First and foremost, write your own introduction. You want to make sure in the intro that you cover the following areas:

1. Who you are;

2. The title of your speech;

3. Why the audience should listen, what's in it for them, and what the speech is about;

4. Your credentials and your expertise on the subject matter; and

5. A lead-in to your topic.

The person introducing you can answer these questions and begin to grab the attention of the audience while creating interest in your subject as well as establishing your credentials. This will help you in your opening.

Here is reality. Your audience is thinking about all sorts of things as you open your mouth. They are not paying attention to you. You are competing with their thoughts. One person may be thinking about the fight they had with their spouse, or perhaps the fight they are planning to have when they get home. Another may be mentally balancing their check book. One may be watching the nice-looking lady on the other aisle. When we speak, we do have competition. We must be more interesting than the woman across the aisle.

It is our job as professional speakers to get their attention before introducing our theme. "Okay," you say, "But Charlie, I am not a professional speaker." I beg to differ with you. If you are giving speeches and you want to do a great job, you need to start considering yourself a professional. Being professional is synonymous with being excellent. Personal Excellence is created in preparation, and that's what sets professionals apart.

Have you ever noticed that a professional speaker will open by talking about something unique about the city in which he finds himself? It could be the football team and a recent victory. It could be the weather. It might be a current event on the national stage. One of my favorite experts on leadership, John Maxwell, will typically start off with a joke or a story. He does not rush his opening. It appears to me that he does not jump into his material until he feels a connection with his audience. My Pastor, Alan Clayton, Senior Pastor of the Ark Church in Conroe, Texas, says that the shortest distance between two hearts is laughter—and it's also one of the quickest ways to grab the audience's attention during a speaking engagement.

> "The shortest distance between two hearts is laughter."
>
> Alan Clayton, Sr. Pastor of The Ark Church

I like organization and logic, and therefore I like an opening that not only grabs the attention of the audience but has a logical flow moving into the theme. You can get there with jokes, humor, or stories that are related to the theme. The opening attention grabber should be somewhat connectable to your theme so that you can easily transition to your theme. For instance, this last sentence about transitioning to your theme is my transition to talk about the theme.

The Opening – Introduce the Theme

The theme is one of the most important parts of a speech. It is like that straw man that we set up in the beginning so that we can tear him down. In order to introduce our theme, we must know what the theme is. Try this exercise: Ask yourself the question, "If I were to boil the message of my speech or presentation down into one sentence, what would it be?" The answer to this question will reveal your theme. Your theme is the core concept or the central message of your presentation.

One of the worst mistakes a speaker can make is to open the speech and not give the audience an idea of where he is heading. People are distracted when your speech leaves something for them to guess. For instance, if in your opening you were to simply say, "I am going to share some thoughts with you today on motorcycling," the questions that would go through the minds of audience's are, "What about motorcycling? Is he going to talk about safety? Is he going to talk about the joy of riding? Is he going to talk about the maintenance of the bike? Is he going to compare bikes?"

Always make sure your audience knows where you are going. You may ask, "What is the harm of letting them guess?" The harm is that if they are guessing, they are distracted and missing some of your message. A more effective opening might be...

"How many of you men would agree with me that every time you go out, you are usually late because you are waiting for your wife to get ready? Now you love your wife, she is a joy, and the waiting is a frustration you are willing to endure. Riding a bike is much the same—it provides much joy, but there is a frustrating downside. Today, I want to share with you the extraordinary maintenance that is required to enjoy riding a bike." With this opening, the audience knows exactly what I am going to speak about. Their minds create a bookshelf to store this information. Now that they are attentive and open to hearing your message, it is time to transition to the body.

The Body

The theme of the speech should run through the body like a backbone. Each and every point has to support the theme and must be attached to the backbone like a vertebra.

While planning to move from the theme to the body, you should design a transition that allows you to easily slide from the introduction of the theme to the first point. In fact, the audience should not even realize that this transition has been made. Let's continue our motorcycle speech and create a transition. Assume our first point in maintaining a motorcycle is the cleaning and detailing.

"Men, those of you who have to wait on your wives to get ready, what do you think they are doing behind closed doors?"

Allow the audience to respond or go ahead and answer the question. It really depends on how much time you have for interaction. If you have time, this would be a great opportunity to plan for some spontaneity. The audience will have fun chiming in.

"I'll tell you what they are doing. First, they are scrubbing off all the old make-up so they can apply a new coat. Then they wash and blowdry their hair. Then comes the nail polish, the fresh coat of makeup, and every shoe in the closet is tried on twice because you are not convincing when you tell her which pair looks best. It is all about fresh polish and accessorizing. I have news for you. We bikers are "faaar" worse! The maintenance item closest to every biker's heart is freshly polished chrome and leather tassels!"

In this transition, I have gone from waiting on wives to get ready (common ground) to my first point, cleaning the bike. Waiting on wives is not important in and of itself. But it does serve as a "twist." This is where I use a more concrete, relatable concept to establish a point, and then I twist it to represent a more abstract or less relatable concept. Many may even miss the humor because of their initial distraction. I would rather them miss this than miss my theme. The good thing is that if I get a laugh out of this or even an "all for fun" boo from the ladies, this will help to reel in the less attentive.

When folks hear the laughing, they begin to tune in. I tried to connect with common ground and humor. Ladies, we could have used an analogy with men and their guns or TV remote controls. Maybe I will do this in the next book. This is how we plan success into a speech.

As you go through your points, follow the same process for transitioning from one point to the other. Each of the points must support the theme and, at the same time, should be moving toward a logical conclusion. The better we set up the theme and the better we can support it, the more effective we can be in boiling the entire presentation down to a logical conclusion.

Logical Conclusion

The conclusion should support and summarize the body and theme. In fact, it is called a logical conclusion because the audience should have already arrived at the conclusion even before you state it. You have one last opportunity to drive your message home.

I chose to talk about the building of a speech because it is a perfect example of something that needs tremendous planning. It is also the one area that can catapult your career and financial status to the next level. Finally, public speaking is a perfect example of something that will stretch us—when you step outside of your comfort zone, you naturally grow.

Bringing the Masterpiece Together

Building the Masterpiece requires preparation through planning, even in designing a speech. The Masterpiece happens in a speech when we create an attention-grabbing opening, brilliantly introduce our theme, smoothly transition into our body and glide from one point to the next, and then boil the entire presentation down to a thick, juicy, and succulent logical conclusion. This is Preparation through Planning, and it leaves you with an economy of words that are rich with substance. We really have **Crossed That Bridge…BEFORE We Get There!** It is only in planning that we create Personal Excellence.

When we create and give speeches or presentations, we do them not because they are easy but because they are hard, and because **that goal (the endeavor of giving a speech) serves to organize and measure the best of our energies and skills.**

Let's take this a step further; if you are really interested in improving your communication and leadership skills, you should consider Toastmasters International. Remember Aristotle? He said, "We are what we repeatedly do; therefore excellence is a habit and not an act.

If we give speeches and presentations periodically, the process is more like an act. Toastmasters offers an opportunity to create excellence through the habit of speaking and leading. You can learn more about Toastmasters International and the local districts at: www.toastmasters.org.

I have seen individuals join Toastmasters, struggle through the first speech, and by speech six, they are getting promotions, raises, better jobs, and changing careers.

I have been a Toastmaster for 10 years and it has tremendously benefitted me in my career and my personal life. I joined to get some much-needed help and discovered soon thereafter that I enjoyed helping others succeed. Toastmasters Communication Track taught me the mechanics of speaking. The Leadership Track transformed me from mere Speaker to Messenger. In the Leadership Track, I was required to give speeches to motivate members and clubs and this gave my words PURPOSE. Purpose creates passion and passion creates energy.

We have discussed the process of preparation through planning so far. If we were race car drivers, this chapter puts us into third gear. We have the competence, power, and skill to get out on the race track and mix it up with the other drivers. We will ramp up to fourth gear in Chapter 3, where we discuss "Painting the Picture of Success." This is where we begin to really shine bright. In Chapter 4, we will ramp up into fifth gear and discuss "Creating and Finding Purpose." This is where we begin to move out in front of the pack. In Chapter 5, we discuss the marketability of our achievements. Finally, Chapter 6 is a special message for salespeople.

Golden Nugget: Purpose creates passion and passion creates energy.

Golden Nuggets and Quotes:

- "In my preparing for battle I have always found that plans are useless, but planning is indispensable." Dwight D. Eisenhower

- "Good plans shape good decisions. That's why good planning helps to make elusive dreams come true." Lester R. Bittel

- Planning turns dreams into visions. It transforms ideas into goals. It puts feet to our desires. And it creates Sustainable Confidence, resulting in Sustainable Success.

- We do not have to depend on being lucky. We can make our journey one of planning and our destiny one of Success.

- If you do not intend to mow, then you do not need a lawnmower. If Michael Jackson never endeavored to sing or dance, that raw and pure talent would have existed only in seed form.

- Our values will be an anchor amidst the storms of temptation.

- We would never be compromise our values if lived up to the character that our dogs think we have.

- A guilty conscience is a cancer that erodes the very foundation of our confidence.

- We can do anything we set our guilt-free minds to. Guilt and worry fertilize the weeds in our minds. A pure conscience is the foundation of a confidence. Confidence is the fruit of a pure conscience.

- "Holding unforgiveness is like eating rat poison … and waiting for the rat to die."   Joe McGee

- "The single biggest problem in communication is the illusion that it has taken place." George Bernard Shaw

- "The art of communication is the language of leadership." James Humes

- Mastering the art of communication is the fastest bridge to promotion and more pay.

- Great communication starts with great planning.

- Rudeness is a weak man's strength. Erick Hoffer

- We judge ourselves by our intentions and we judge others by that they do. John C. Maxwell.

- "The shortest distance between two hearts is laughter." Alan Clayton, Sr. Pastor of The Ark Church

- Purpose creates passion, and passion creates energy.

Notes Page:

Reference	Page No.

We have framed the backdrop with planning, now let's...

Paint the Picture of Success

CHAPTER 3

PAINTING THE PICTURE OF SUCCESS

"Formulate a stamp indelibly on your mind a mental picture of yourself as succeeding. Hold this picture tenaciously. Never permit it to fade. Your mind will seek to develop the picture...Do not build obstacles in your imagination."

Norman Vincent Peale

Let me add to what the legendary Dr. Peale said. Your mind will develop the picture <u>and your body converts it into the motion picture</u>. If we spend the proper time in Planning and painting the Picture of success, then we can show up and allow the movie to begin.

I learned this concept totally by accident. Many years ago when I was younger and had a flat belly, my brother-in-law and I would play basketball one-on-one. Don was a much better basketball player than I was. He was actually talented. However, I had something going for me as well. I was a hard worker. Because of my hard work and hustle, the scores were fairly even.

One Saturday morning we were playing the best two out of three games. It was no contest; he was taking me to school. Every time I made one of my signature moves toward the goal, he would take the ball away from me and he would score. None of my "World Famous" moves were working that day. I was down two games and was on my way to losing my third game. I kept asking myself what was different. Did I wake up on the wrong side of the bed or the wrong side of the universe?

I had the ball and was trying to come up with an approach, but had little to no motivation left. I did not know what to do and was contemplating taking a shot from half court—maybe even a granny shot...I had a better chance of scoring from there than I did trying to slip him for a layup. As I looked up at the goal I began to picture the ball going in. I kept my eyes on the goal and kept the picture in my mind. I made my move keeping my eyes on the goal. Like magic, my body somehow was able find a way around Don and to get to the goal. Wow! I focused on my goal, my mind developed the picture, and my body converted it into a motion picture. What a valuable lesson I learned that day—I had painted a Picture of Success. It was like magic! My failure was created by focusing on my obstacle. I realized I had been watching Don. I did not need to focus on what was in my way; I needed to focus on my destination. My success was created by having a vivid picture of the goal and the ball going in.

In my message to the reader in the front of this book, I mentioned that our circumstances and experiences tend to determine our limitations. While I focused on Don as an obstacle between me and the goal, my mind developed a picture of prevention. I had the wrong picture. Our mind thinks in pictures and follows them as a road map. Here is the good news. We can paint over those old pictures. We can paint a new picture.

Golden Nugget: When circumstances and bad experiences have spray-painted graffiti in the corridors of our minds, we are absolutely permitted to paint over those negative messages with our own pictures of success.

I am reminded of an experiment that was done some time ago. This experiment has been talked about for years. It consisted of two basketball teams that were to play. One team practiced very hard physically. The other team sat around in the evenings and envisioned the shots they were going to be making. They only prepared mentally.

Guess what? They showed up and allowed the motion picture to begin. The team with mental preparation soundly defeated the team that had prepared physically. This is not to say that physical preparation is not necessary. It is very necessary. Both teams were in the middle of a season and had been preparing physically for quite some time. The difference was that the winning team focused on Painting a Picture of Success for this particular game and set the motion picture rolling.

Let's use another example: focusing ahead, rather than on the immediate, to aid your journey to success. I used to love to jog. I found that as I fatigued my eyes would drop to the ground. My pace would slow. As I looked to the horizon, my pace would pick up.

When taking the motorcycle safety course, they teach you when navigating around a long curve, look at the straight away beyond the curve. In other words, look at the horizon where you are heading or look at your destiny. You are not supposed to look at the curve because you will overcompensate.

The lesson from these two anecdotes: keep your eye on the goal and not on the obstacle.

Golden Nugget: Where we focus with our mental and physical eyes will determine to a large degree our Success.

Great men of different eras, including Socrates, Aristotle, Descartes, and Einstein, all believed that we create the world we live in through our thoughts.

We have discussed Preparation through Planning in Chapter 2. We are now focusing on preparing mentally through painting the Picture of Success. We have shifted to fourth gear! Let's gain some speed with a real-life experience.

In 1989, I started a new job. I was in charge of the technical aspect of a product line. It was the last day of the month and I found six of the rubber elements palletized and ready for shipment. None of them had been tested, so I began to ask around to find out why.

Finally, the person responsible for testing pulled me aside and told me that he was told to bypass the test, because it was the last day of the month and they needed the shipments to make budget. After hearing this, I put a hold tag on the elements. The placement of these little yellow tags was akin to pulling the detonator pins on grenades. I started a major series of explosions. From that day forward, the production manager came after me personally.

As I walked through the plant, Big Jim, who was usually standing around with production guys, would make me the brunt of the joke. He would shout vulgarities. Every time there were layoffs, he threw my name in the hat and told the management team that I did not really do anything. He even told the CEO of the company that I was getting kickbacks from the machine shops we were using. What an onslaught. He came after me with both barrels.

I was devastated and I lost all confidence. I became indecisive. When others came to me for assistance, I would struggle with what should have been simple decisions. For the first time in my life, I began to believe that I was going to get myself fired. I was acting like an incompetent. And to add insult to injury, I was teaming up with Big Jim to get me fired. *"We"* were now ganging up on me—not just him. I like what Eleanor Roosevelt said: "No one can make us feel inferior without our consent." What was I to do?

> No one can make you feel inferior without your consent.   Eleanor Roosevelt

After a fierce internal struggle, I made the decision to affirm myself. I was no longer going to give my consent and team up with Big Jim. I decided to team up with "Charming Charlie." Remember that the only part of the Success equation for which I had control was the preparation portion. I did not know at the time what I was doing, but I used the paintbrush of my tongue to paint a Picture of Success. I began to talk to myself every morning. Every morning I would say:

- Charlie, your head is screwed on straight. You are confident and decisive. You know what you are doing.

- Charlie, you are good at what you do. In fact, you are the best tool designer in the entire United States.

- Charlie, as a matter of fact, you are so good at what you do, people are going to start bypassing your boss and come directly to you for solutions.

As ridiculous as the last confession sounds, well, all I can say is, "Be careful how you affirm yourself." Here is the funny and incredible part. Within two weeks, I had so many people coming directly to me that a memo was distributed forbidding people from bypassing my boss and coming directly to me. It addressed the fact that my boss scheduled my work. After two more weeks, they were coming directly to me again.

Here is the even funnier part. A few years down the road, I had a boss say that he would match my design talents against anyone in the nation. I excelled in the areas where I affirmed myself.

Why did this work? It allowed me to weed my garden. At that time, I had a weed problem—my mind was overwhelmed with negativity, and the more I let myself think those thoughts, the more they multiplied. Eventually I was able to change the picture in my mind, and that gave me a tremendous amount of confidence. I developed the picture. My body converted it into a motion picture.

I love what Brian Tracey, a leading trainer of salespeople and an author, teaches. On the way to sales calls, he would repeat out loud, "I like myself. I like myself. I like myself." What was he doing? He was affirming himself. When we are happy with who we are and we like what we are doing and what we stand for, others like us. Have you ever noticed that folks who are not very well liked don't seem to like themselves very much? If we don't like ourselves, it is hard to send the message to others that we are worthy of liking. We project to others what we feel about ourselves.

Remember, no matter what picture that our circumstance has painted on our brains and no matter how we feel, we can paint a new picture over the old one. It is amazing that when we paint picture vivid and vibrant enough, others can see it as well.

Dale Carnegie, in his book *How to Win Friends and Influence People*, tells the story of his interview with Howard Thurston. Mr. Thurston was a magician and enjoyed a 40-year career practicing his magic for more than 60 million people across the world. This earned him a two million dollar profit. He was much more successful than his counterparts, and Carnegie asked him the secret to his success.

They had to rule out his education. As a child he ran away from home and lived as a hobo riding the boxcars. In fact, he learned to read by looking out the boxcars at the signs. They had to rule out his knowledge, as the magicians all studied from the same books. Mr. Thurston explained that there were two things he did differently. One was his preparation. He practiced and timed every word, gesture and facial expression. **He Crossed That Bridge...BEFORE He Got There.** The second difference was his feelings for the audience. The other magicians would say, "Well, there is a bunch of suckers out there, a bunch of hicks; I will fool them all right."

Thurston would say, "I am grateful because these people come to see me. They make it possible for me to make my living in a very agreeable way. I am going to give them the very best I possibly can." The key here is that the audience picked up on his appreciation. He painted a vivid and vibrant picture about liking his audience that his audience was able to see as well.

Our obstacles are communicating that we cannot do this or do that. In many cases they have painted graffiti in the corridors of our minds. Have you ever wondered why the circus workers can contain a full grown elephant with a small rope tied to his leg and the other end to a stake in the ground? The reason for this is that they start training the elephants when the elephants are babies. The trainers use a large chain attached to a post cemented into the ground. The elephant struggles until he is convinced that he cannot break loose. At that point, the trainers can use a rope and a stake. Circumstances have painted graffiti in the elephant's mind that communicates a message of bondage.

There was another experiment done years ago that involved an aquarium of fish. The main meal of these fish was guppies. For this experiment, the guppies were put into a smaller aquarium, and it was lowered partially into the larger tank. The fish would lunge toward the guppies and bounce off of the glass. After several hours of aggressively attacking to no avail, the fish finally became convinced that they could not get to the guppies and they quit trying. The circumstances created graffiti in their minds that communicated that guppies were off limits.

The second phase of the experiment was to dump the guppies into the aquarium with the fish. The fish were convinced that they could not get to the guppies, and therefore the guppies were able to swim feed-frenzy-free. The obstacles of the fish communicated, "You are not able to eat these guppies." If the guppies had been dumped into the aquarium before the first experiment was done, the fish would not have believed they were unable to eat the guppies. Wow! How much more nourished they would have been if no one convinced them they could not eat guppies.

I am reminded of the story of when Dr. Norman Vincent Peale was visiting Hong Kong. Many of you may have heard of the book *Think and Grow Rich.* In addition to authoring this book, Dr. Peale was a tremendous motivational speaker. He saw a Chinese tattoo parlor and was admiring the artwork in the window. One piece of artwork caught his attention. It simply read, "Born to Lose." In astonishment, he entered the parlor. He asked the owner, "Does anyone really have that terrible phrase, 'Born to Lose,' tattooed on his body?" The tattoo artist replied, "Yes, sometimes." "But," Dr. Peale said, "I just can't believe that anyone in his right mind would do that." The Chinese man simply tapped his forehead and said in broken English, "Before tattoo on body, tattoo on mind." Yes, the graffiti in the corridors of our minds does translate into success or failure. What we believe in our minds is externalized.

Let me ask a question. What if we were unaware that we were not supposed to be able to do something? How would that impact our ability? Have you heard George Dantzig's story? George was a doctrinal candidate at the University of California, Berkeley, in 1939. He arrived to class late and saw two math problems on the board. He thought that the two problems were part of the homework assignment. He jotted them down, and that evening he solved them. He did not realize that during the time before he arrived to class, the professor introduced these two problems with the class as unsolvable problems. He was not privy to the conversation that said, "You are unable to solve these problems." He ate the guppies. He actually solved both problems.

When we paint a picture of success, we become guppy eaters. It is true. We can do anything we put our guilt-free mind to. Painting a picture of success is vital to **Crossing That Bridge...BEFORE We Get There.**

Friends and Fellow Guppy Eaters, allow me to let you in on a secret. You may or may not get accolades and praises when you do a good job. We know that people are motivated more by recognition than money. Therefore, you need to give yourself accolades and praises. He who toots not his own horn, it gets not tooted. You do not have to toot it to others; if you just develop the picture in your mind, your body will convert it into a motion picture. Let's paint the picture bold and vibrant so that others can see it too.

By the way, I wish to thank Big Jim now for the valuable lesson he helped me to learn about Painting the Picture of Success. Thanks Jim! I promise I did not eat any rat poison...well, maybe just a little, but I am forever grateful for the lesson learned.

Painting a Picture for Success in Public Speaking

We spoke in Chapter 2 about the importance of

planning when it comes to speaking one-on-one, public speaking, or giving presentations. Here is the key. After taking the platform, we have no more time to prepare. It is done. The only thing we carry on to the platform with us is the picture that we develop in our minds. If we are going to step on the platform and allow the movie to begin, we must prepare by planning and then converting that to a picture of success. Fellow Guppy Eaters, we never feel totally prepared. If not careful, that message of not feeling completely prepared will paint a picture of worry and failure. Let's finish our preparation by painting the Picture of Success.

If we do not create a picture, our minds will create their own picture. Your mind will create pictures like:

- What if I forget my speech?

- What if I don't connect with the audience?

- What if they don't like me?

- What if they ask questions that I don't know the answer to?

- What if I freeze?

These are fast-growing weeds. We must create our own pictures or the weeds will take over. Before I speak, I always ask myself, "Why am I doing this and what outcome do I desire?" Answering these questions helps me to determine my purpose, which also helps me develop my picture. If my answer is that this speaking engagement is a good opportunity for exposure, then I must find a purpose greater than that. We always have to have a purpose bigger than ourselves.

Once I have a purpose to carry my message, then I can begin to paint the picture.

- I am speaking because I have a life-changing message. This is a divine appointment and I am here for a reason. This is less about me and more about my audience. I am going to motivate someone today. Someone may be about to give up. They need to hear what I have.

- I picture myself smiling and confident. When I physically prepare, I physically smile big. I create a vivid image of me smiling. In fact, I put Joel Osteen's smile on my face.

- I picture myself making grand but natural gestures.

- I picture myself capitalizing on the responses of the audience. In fact, when I am reading through my material, I look for possible audience reactions and plan the "impromptu" response. Yes, it is true, improvisation is not improv, and it is very much planned or at least thought about ahead of time.

- I picture electrifying energy. I need a purpose big enough to create big passion.

This is vital. When I hit the stage, the only thing I carry with me is the Picture of Success. We never feel totally prepared. If we think we are, our minds will have the last laugh. Never apologize for forgetting something. Never apologize for messing up part of your speech. ***No one has ever heard the speech that you MEANT to*** *give!* If you do not tell them you messed up or forgot part of your speech, they will never know. If proper planning has been done and a strong picture of success has been painted, then the picture will carry you when you forget or mess up on parts of your presentation. Painting a Picture of Success is necessary in all types of communication, including one-on-one.

Painting a Picture of Success: One-on-One

Day in and day out, we are creating success or failure through our communications. We have to communicate with our spouse, our children, our boss, and our coworkers.

> Communication - the human connection - is the key to personal and career success.
> Paul J. Meyer

Properly setting up the conversation is critical. We talked in Chapter 2 about proper preparation through planning. Again, once the conversation has started, it is the painted picture that will take over and create the motion picture.

Years ago, the GM of our company, to whom I reported, jumped my inside sales gal in front of others. She was highly intelligent, very task driven, but tended to treat people like tasks as well. She needed information and apparently pushed the GM's last button, and he subsequently unloaded on her. She was devastated. I went into see her and she was crying uncontrollably.

It is always good to wait 24 hours before responding when you are angry, and I did just that. I had to deal with this in a way that ensured it would not happen again. In my planning, some of the elements that I deemed important for my approach were:

- I needed to be calm and not angry. Anger begets anger.

- I needed to be non-critical and promote understanding. Criticism initiates defense mechanisms.

- I needed to follow Stephen Covey's advice: "Seek first to understand before seeking to be understood." By the way, he who asks questions controls the conversation. If you ever find yourself in a heated discussion, ask questions. This keeps the faucet open on the other party and allows you collect your thoughts and to tailor your responses on the fly. You know who was a master at this: It was Columbo, played by Peter Falk, in the television detective mystery series from 1971 through 2003. Columbo would pretend dumb and ask a lot of questions. People took him for harmless and would talk enough to incriminate themselves.

- I needed some assurance that this would never happen again. I wanted action.

What outcome did I want? I wanted to put a preemptive end to any future spontaneous outbursts.

I spent the time preparing on paper, and then I began painting my picture. I put on my game face. I pictured myself as open and interested in hearing his side while stern about making sure it never happened again. I pictured myself as confident and in control. This was vital because this conversation could go south quickly. I made an appointment and also told him what I wanted to talk about. This gave him a chance to prepare as well.

When we sat down to speak, I started the conversation off on a lighter note about some other items and then transitioned into the topic. Why did I start the conversation off on a lighter note? I needed to make a connection on a civil level to communicate that life is still normal, and this was not the end of the world. I needed to communicate that I was not angry. I also needed to gage his mindset and locate my audience. Great communication starts with the speaker meeting his audience on common ground and then leading them down the desired path. Again, remember the professional speaker and how he begins talking about the local football team, or some recent event, or something unique about the city. He wants to corral the audience's minds and get their attention before jumping into his material. Always locate your audience and meet them where they are.

After the initial greeting and some conversation on a lighter note, I stated there was the incident the other day with Gail. I asked him to help me understand what exactly happened and why. He stated that she kept pushing him on a delivery and not giving him time to gather the information. He said she was relentless and she just got to him. I sympathized with him regarding her bulldog tenacity but also told him if he ever need to vent at someone to vent at me, and I would deal with her.

He said it should not have happened. This was great. He was moving toward my desired outcome. I had not exercised anger. I did not criticize or accuse. This was my opportunity to communicate sternness. I stated that I agreed that it should not have happened, and I continued that it could never happen again. He said he would try. I was looking for something more definite, along the lines of "Charlie, I agree with you and it will never happen again." I did not get that, so I repeated that it could never happen again. I received the same response. After the third attempt with the same response, I realized that this was as good as it was going to get. We were at a stalemate, but I had communicated what I needed to. And in his own way, he took responsibility for what he had done and assured me it was his intention to not let it happen again. We may not always get the outcome we expected, but we need to recognize a "win" when we have it. I thanked him for his time and went on. My picture of success allowed me to keep my cool when I did not get the total results I wanted.

This may not seem like much of a conversation, but remember this was my boss. It was also an individual who had much different philosophies than I did, which caused us to butt heads often. Trust me; this conversation had the potential to be volatile. In fact, in our younger and less mature days, we did have volatile conversations. The one thing that I really admired about this individual is that in spite of our differences, he did not hold a grudge. I never knew him to eat rat poison. We could lock horns, and five minutes later we were talking about fishing. We were so different that in many ways we complemented and balanced one another. And we accomplished some great goals together.

When you work with folks who are very different than yourself, preparation with communication is vital. It can be the difference between a stalemate and accomplishing great things together.

The point to this story is that I was able to accomplish a reasonable outcome by preparing on paper, then developing the picture of what Success looked like in my mind. The efforts to prepare through planning and developing the picture in my mind allowed me to show up and start the motion picture. That particular day, I enjoyed a mess of guppies.

You may have noticed that many of the questions we ask ourselves during the planning portion are actually driven by purpose. We are now ready to shift into fifth gear and begin to lead the pack.

Golden Nuggets and Quotes:

- "Formulate a stamp indelibly on your mind, a mental picture of yourself as succeeding. Hold this picture tenaciously. Never permit it to fade. Your mind will seek to develop the picture.... Do not build obstacles in your imagination." Dr. Norman Vincent Peale

- When circumstances and bad experiences have spray-painted graffiti in the corridors of our minds, we are absolutely permitted to paint over those negative messages with our own pictures of success.

- Where we focus with our mental and physical eyes will determine to a large degree our Success.

- "No one can make you feel inferior without your consent." Eleanor Roosevelt

- "Communication—the human connection—is the key to personal and career success." Paul J. Meyer

Notes Page:

Reference	Page No.

More people succeed through PURPOSE than through talent. —*Charlie   Pitts*

CHAPTER 4

PURPOSE

> *"More men fail through a lack of purpose than a lack of talent."*
>
> *William Ashley*

The most effective skill is that which is slow cooked in the roué of raw talent. It is only when we begin stretching ourselves and reaching for our personal moon that our talent begins to take root and allows us to fully develop our skill sets. Just as Leadership provides purpose to our words and causes us to move from Speaker to Messenger, purpose is the fuel for achievers. As William Ashley stated, people do not fail for a lack of talent as much as they do for lack of purpose.

Golden Nugget: Purpose is the fuel of achievers.

Even when one lacks talent and does little to prepare through planning and little to picture success, purpose seems to pull that person through. Think about the late, great Mother Teresa. This was a simple woman. She was not a great communicator. Nor was she a skilled business woman. Yet look at what she was able to accomplish! Blessed Teresa of Calcutta said in her biography,

"By blood I am an Albanian. By citizenship, an Indian. By faith, I am a Catholic nun. As to my calling, I belong to the world. As to my heart, I belong entirely to the Heart of Jesus."

She created the Missionaries of Charity. At the time of her death, the organization consisted of 610 missions in 123 countries. In 2012 after her death, it consisted of 4,500 sisters in 133 countries. The 4,500 sisters are vowed to "To give Wholehearted and Free service to the poorest of the poor." She built a gigantic charity organization on pure purpose.

The most important thing we can do is to have purpose in our endeavors. This gives rise to the question, "Charlie, if this was so important, why wasn't if first on the list?" That is a good question, and I am glad you asked.

The reason for not having it first is that it does not always come first. A favorite scripture of mine says, "Your Word is a lamp unto my feet and a light unto my path." Please take a journey with me. Picture the old oil–burning lanterns that folks used to use. The lantern would throw out a dim light around their feet. It was truly a lamp around their feet, but nothing more. In order to see a trail or a pathway, they would have to walk. It is only in action that our paths became clear. Sometimes purpose is not realized until we are deep within the planning stages or even in the execution stages.

Golden Nugget: It is only in action that our paths become clear.

Sometimes we know the purpose and we know why we are driven to do something. Other times, we feel compelled to do something and learn our purpose in the process. Yet in other instances, we have been asked to do something and we have no control over the process or the input. Here is where we have to create or find a purpose.

Finding Purpose in Projects

Many times we are given projects and do not see the value. In fact, we "know" they are a waste of time: "Why on earth would management waste my time?" How you handle these issues will determine your ability to move up. Remember, more men have failed due to a lack of purpose than a lack of talent. Here are some possible thoughts to help find purpose:

- Perhaps management also believes the project is not worth continuing and they need confirmation. You are the person in the trenches. You are the person with the expertise and they trust your professional opinion.

- Maybe you have no clue why management wants you to do the research and present the report. But know this; the quality of your work will have a definite impact on your career. It will impact it positively or negatively. Pause...digest this for a moment. To do poor quality work will negatively impact your career. To do excellent work will positively impact your career. Here is where we can create purpose and say, "I am ecstatic that I have been entrusted with this project. I am going to do the best job I possibly can. I am going to showcase my talents and gifts." Okay, you say, "Charlie, my company never recognizes talent or a good job. It will make no difference because they don't know the difference." Fair enough, but you know the difference. Doing the right thing and creating Personal Excellence creates Sustainable Confidence and Sustainable Success. Doing excellent work will create achievements and prepare you for your next job.

Golden Nugget: I am always preparing for my next promotion or my next job.

- Perhaps your management is testing you. Maybe they want to further utilize you and are testing your professional skills or your entrepreneurial skills.

- Maybe you have been given a canned

presentation and you have no control over the boring materials. It is important that we take ownership of the material and create a little passion over the presentation. It may not be your material, but once you present it, it has your signature on it. We must create Personal Excellence through planning, painting the Picture of Success, and bathing it in Purpose.

Companies do not promote people. We promote ourselves by becoming. We are not fakers, we are becomers. It is vital to have purpose in everything we do, and this will allow us to give it our best effort and our best energy. This purpose may have to be discovered, or it may have to be created.

Purpose in Public Speaking

If there is not purpose behind your speech you will have no passion or energy. If there is no purpose, you will not be committed to the material. One of the key ingredients that keeps people's attention is your energy.

Part of the reason that the fear of public speaking ranks consistently in the top three is that the focus is on us. Purpose is the catalyst for confidence. The larger the purpose, the less we focus on ourselves.

Golden Nugget: Purpose is the catalyst for confidence.

Let me illustrate purpose with an analogy. I realize that the analogy that I have chosen is based on a sensitive subject matter. I do not want to make light of this for

Cross That Bridge…BEFORE You Get There

those whose lives have been affected by drunk drivers. Having stated that, this is a very powerful analogy and I feel it best illustrates the point.

Deloris was a little frail housewife. She spent her life taking care of her husband and five children. She volunteered for the PTA; she was a den mother and a team mom throughout the years. However, she would always avoid positions that required public speaking or even speaking to the group. She was happy just to be invisible in the background. She was terrified of public speaking.

One day tragedy struck. Her family was impacted by a drunk driver. Going forward six months, there was a congressional hearing on drunk drivers and MADD (Mothers Against Drunk Driving) was there to testify. It was a large event and was covered by CSPAN. The lady who spoke on behalf of MADD was articulate and passionate. She was demonstrative. She spoke with confidence, courage, and boldness. What happened to Deloris that made her into such a powerful speaker over night? She got PURPOSE. She did not have a speech. She had a MESSAGE! She was the Messenger. It was not about her but about a big purpose.

Purpose was the catalyst for her courage and confidence. Purpose has the ability to transform us.

Golden Nugget: Purpose transforms us from Speaker to Messenger.

When you have the privilege of giving a speech or a

presentation and you invest the time in Preparation by planning, painting a Picture of what Success looks like, and bathing it in Purpose, you are on your way to being a powerful, motivational speaker who will be invited back...and very possibly get paid for it.

If you apply the three P's of success to your values, your work, your projects, and your communication, you are on your way to creating Personal Excellence and increasing your value to the company for which you work.

Golden Nugget: More people succeed through PURPOSE than through talent.

Golden Nuggets and Quotes:

- "More men fail though a lack of purpose than a lack of talent." William Ashley

- It was only in action that our paths became clear.

- I am always preparing for my next promotion or my next job.

- Purpose is the fuel of achievers.

- Purpose is the catalyst for confidence.

- Purpose transforms us from Speaker to Messenger.

- "More people succeed through Purpose than through talent." Charlie Pitts

Notes Page:

Reference	Page No.

Let's pull it all together and discuss

the Marketable Benefits for:

Crossing That Bridge…

BEFORE We Get There.

Chapter 5

IT'S MARKETABLE

> *"Give and it shall be given to you."*
>
> *Luke 6:38*

Relax, I mentioned a scripture, but I am not going to preach to you. People of faith understand this scripture. Others may know the old cliché, "What goes around, comes around." It is also called the law of reciprocity.

Why is this concept important? If you endeavor to reach for your personal moon, chances are you will want to engage in volunteer activities outside of your career. "But Charlie," you say, "I'm already so busy—why on earth would I want to devote time I don't have to volunteering?" My answer: the benefits are overwhelming, both from a self-interested standpoint and from an altruistic one. I have learned more about leadership, motivation, communication, and people psychology while volunteering than I have on the job. Even though I learned off the job, the lessons were transferrable and beneficial to my career. And here is the kicker: The talents you develop and the skills you learn while volunteering are marketable. The leadership and communication skills you gain are priceless.

I have volunteered in some form or fashion for the past 30 years. In addition to the awakening of talents within me and the development of skills, I have accomplished many things. When we volunteer, we create achievements. Get a load of this:

Golden Nugget: We market our ability by demonstrating our achievement.

I am not sure you heard me.

Golden Nugget: We market our ability by demonstrating our achievement.

This is a vital statement. We have discussed that companies do not promote us. We promote ourselves by demonstrating our achievements. Your job may be mundane and you think no one is watching. I would bet that someone is watching. Even if no one were watching, your own conscience is watching. Taking pride in our work and knowing that we gave it our best and did a great job creates satisfaction and confidence.

Remember, you are preparing for your next promotion or your next job.

In 1996, good friends of mine decided to start a church in Conroe, Texas, where I lived and worked. I was out of church but decided I would show up to the grand opening to honor an old friend. (I had already worked with those friends, Pastors Alan and Joy Clayton, in the singles ministry at Lakewood Church, in Houston, Texas, in the early- to mid-80s). I accepted the invitation, showed up at the first service, and Pastors Alan and Joy put me to work ushering—and I stayed.

During that time, I was working in the engineering discipline and wanted to move to sales. My friends told me this would be difficult. I had no experience. I had no track record. I had no training. I was told that if I wanted to be in sales, I would probably have to take an entry level position and a large cut in pay. This advice was correct and the observations were sound. In fact, anyone who knew me then knew that I was not a good candidate for sales at the time. In addition to not having the skill set, I was a "hot-head." Here is the key to my eventual transition: I became a guppy eater. I began to paint over the graffiti and tattoos. I started a journey of becoming.

Let's take a break from the story for a moment and talk about "faking it" versus "becoming." I mentioned in Chapter 1 that I have a problem with "fake it till you make it." I understand what my colleagues mean when they use it. They are simply saying that if you don't feel like doing something, do it and the feeling will come. If you don't feel like smiling but you do it anyway, the feeling will come. Many, however, use this cliché to justify not preparing and then trying to pretend they are something they are not. They try to operate with confidence not yet generated. They are building the foundation of their confidence on quicksand.

But confidence does not come by faking it. It comes by doing the things that build confidence. Excellence does not come by faking it. It comes by doing. Remember what Aristotle said: "We are what we repeatedly do, therefore excellence is a habit, not an act." I am all for picturing success. That is what this book is about...but only if the journey to success and the actions taken in pursuit thereof are supported by the pillars of planning. If it is not supported by the pillars of planning, it could be a fatal failure.

I propose that we replace "fake it till you make it" with "emulate until you assimilate."

Golden Nugget: Emulate until you assimilate.

The definition for Emulate:

- To strive to equal;

- To equal or to approach equality with.

It is a far better approach to say "I am striving to become" as opposed to saying "I am faking it" or creating an act. We do not want to become an actor.

111

The definition of assimilate:

- To take in and utilize as nourishment. Absorb into the system;

- To take into mind and thoroughly understand;

- To make similar.

The word "assimilate" indicates that we are taking ownership. When we STRIVE to equal, the word strive indicates action. When there is action, the gifts and talents that are in seed form begin to sprout and blossom and bloom. We take in and utilize action as nourishment. And the end result is that we become. Emulate until we assimilate!

Golden Nugget: Repeat to yourself: I am a BECOMER and not a faker.

Let's continue my original story. Pastor Alan put me to work ushering. As the church congregation grew, I coordinated the efforts of the greeters, security, the parking lot, and the ushers. I found myself feeling so inadequate and unsure. Pastor Alan gave me a book by John Maxwell, *Developing the Leader Within You*, and I read it. I began to read other books on leadership, people skills, and sales. I put these principles into action and learned leadership. I began to wake up the motivational gifts within me, and at the same time, I learned some valuable skills in dealing with people. Thank you, Pastor Alan, for believing in me and making an investment in my future.

I did not realize it, but the skills that I needed for sales, I actually learned while volunteering at the church. In September of 2000, I was able to change careers without giving up any pay.

I already mentioned that while working as Engineering Manager and volunteering at the church, I determined that I wanted to be in sales despite the skepticism of those who knew me. I needed a challenge that was more interesting than balancing the strengths of materials, and the people challenge was on my radar.

My plan was to learn sales by reading books that I thought salespeople would read. I had never been in sales, and therefore I had no basis for determining what books salespeople would read. My ignorance was definitely bliss, which resulted in me reading a wide range of books that included guides on leadership, self-improvement, purpose, the different closes, and negotiating. This gave me more insight into the strategic side of sales as opposed to just having a tactical knowledge.

I began to observe and emulate successful people. It is noteworthy that I did not just emulate successful salespeople, I embraced the great actions and principles of all successful people I was fortunate enough cross paths with. Also noteworthy, I did not realize that by emulating, I was painting the Picture of Success. I became a salesman, a diplomat and a professional while working as an Engineering Manager.

Prior to moving into sales, I took a job with another

company as a Senior Design Engineer. Two significant things happened during my two years of employment with that company. First, I attended calls with the salesmen to talk about technical issues. I was told by several that I should be in sales. Secondly, I was required to take a profile evaluation. I did and the results stated that I would not be a good candidate for sales. Those that this test identified as being good for sales were Type "A" personalities, ego-driven and extroverted. I am none of the above. I am an introvert who has learned to extrovert.

Six months after taking this profile evaluation, I received a call from my previous boss. He asked if I wanted a job. I politely responded that I have a good job. He said that this one was in sales. I responded, "Like I was saying, when can I start?"

My purpose was strong and it drove me on. I knew I could do more and wanted the opportunity to cut my teeth in sales. In sales, I learned that I had to find or create purpose when having to carry bad news to the customer. One example happened was when I was tasked with doubling the price to a customer. I began to look for ways to create a win/win situation. I discovered that we had a single cavity tool and the customer's quantities now justified a nine-cavity tool. If I divided the set-up time over nine cavities, I was able to mitigate the damage to the customer and increase our company's margin. The customer understood the dilemma and appreciated me bringing options to the table. I was his problem solver. I was able to change my purpose from doubling the price to the customer to bringing options to help him save money.

In the beginning of this journey I allowed circumstances and people to paint graffiti and tattoos in the corridors of my brain, but I learned how to paint over the bad art work. Let's recap some really important points here:

- My gifts and talents were awakened while volunteering.

- Volunteering allowed me to accomplish achievements and to become by practicing the lessons learned in my readings.

- I learned a skill set that helped me change my career.

- I did not just study leadership and people skills, I practiced them at work. I was BECOMING. I was emulating until I could assimilate.

- Companies do not promote employees. Employees promote themselves by becoming, by emulating until they assimilate. I emulated a salesman and BECAME before I was able to move into sales.

- The leadership and people skills learned volunteering were directly transferrable.

- The skills I learned while volunteering were marketable.

Again, we market our ability by demonstrating our

achievement. When I review a résumé, I am looking for achievement. I am as interested in knowing what a person does to volunteer and what he or she has accomplished. I know that if a person can lead a group of volunteers who do not receive a paycheck, then he can lead groups of people who do receive a paycheck.

Give and it shall be given unto you. The scripture continues to read, "For with what measure you use, it will be measured back to you." What I gave while volunteering pales in comparison to what I received.

Say it with me: **"I Will Cross That Bridge...BEFORE I Get There."** If you will invest in proper preparation by always Planning, painting a Picture of Success, and last but not least, bathing your endeavor in Purpose, you will certainly enjoy success and enjoy being out in front of the pack. The journey will allow you to wake up your gifts and talents. The journey will allow you to learn new skill sets. That which you accomplish on your journey is marketable and transferrable.

Golden Nuggets and Quotes:

- Luke 6:38 "Give and it shall be given to you."

- We market our ability by demonstrating our achievement.

- Emulate until you assimilate.

- I am a BECOMER and not a faker.

Notes Page:

Reference	Page No.

A Special Note to Salespeople.

Chapter 6

MISSING INGREDIENTS FOR EFFECTIVE SALES

The encyclopedia salesman! What a trip. I invited him in knowing that he was commission-based, and even though I was not going to buy, I thought I would be polite and give him a break by listening to his spiel. Those type of salespeople have a really tough job.

"It is a beautiful day, isn't it? Wow, take a look at the color of these books. They match your décor, don't they? I see you have an empty book shelf by your fireplace. These would probably fit very nicely, don't you think?" I admired how he used the "mini-close." My rendition is a little choppy, but he was Mr. Smooth. The mini-close is a process of getting the customer to say "yes" on small benign things. This softens the will to say "no" in general.

Yet if he had managed to sell me the set of encyclopedias, it would not have been a good sale. He would have received his commission, but I would have spent a bunch of money on something for which I had no use. I would have had buyer's remorse in the morning.

A successful close is when both parties win. The salespeople who do well today are those who are problem solvers.

> *"You don't close a sale, you open a relationship if you want to build a long-term, successful enterprise."*
> Patricia Fripp

It is far better to find natural commonality and agree on those points as opposed to creating arbitrary questions and coercing the prospects into saying "Yes."

This chapter is short and sweet. What we have covered in the preceding five chapters is 90% of what we need to be successful in sales. In this chapter, we are applying the concept of **Crossing That Bridge...BEFORE We Get There** specifically to the sales approach. We are not going to talk about the specific closes or the different techniques; there are many books available on this subject matter. Instead, we will discuss what I consider to be the missing ingredient. Let's start by discussing traditional salespeople.

Have you ever been to a used car lot and you immediately distrusted the salesperson? You don't even know the guy, but you immediately form a distrust for him.

Chances are he was breathing on you with "commission

breath," meaning that the sale was more important to him than making sure you get what you want or need. And if you hang around long enough, he will pull out all of the sales techniques he has in his bag. This is the traditional salesperson. This style does not create ongoing success. This style is based on archaic paradigms that need to be crushed. These folks have no Emotional Intelligence.

Those of us who are in sales must change our paradigm. Our focus has to shift to one of Solving **Problems** and not closing the deal. I know, this is counter-intuitive, but if we add value by solving the problem, the deal almost closes itself. I am not saying that we don't need to close the deal; I am saying that closing the deal is a process and we cannot shortcut that process. If we start out closing the deal before we have qualified the prospect and given due diligence to the process, then the deal is often CLOSED before we can close it.

If we focus on closing the deal without due process:

1. We do not listen to the customer.

2. We don't find out what the customer needs and what problems are keeping him up at night.

3. We do not come across as genuinely interested in the other person and his or her needs. That person will back away from our commission breath.

4. We are not looking for opportunities to add value.

5. We never connect with our audience.

There is a time to close the deal, but there is a process that gets us there.

> *"Most people think "selling" is the same as "talking".*
> *But the most effective salespeople know that*
> *listening is the most important part of their job."*
>
> Roy Bartell

Much of our time together has been spent talking about communication. Sales is no different. Listening is a key component of communication and is vital to closing the deal. Remember what Stephen Covey said: "Seek first to understand before seeking to be understood." While I think it is important to know the different closes and the different sales techniques, we cannot shortcut the process.

I was given a new account a few years ago and was told by my colleague to check with a particular individual at that company for other contacts. My colleague was close to this individual, so he called and set up the introduction.

I called this client and got his voice message. In the message that I left, I told him that my colleague told me to call so that he could help me with a few names. After several calls with no response, my colleague called to find out what the deal was. I was able to find out that I shortcut the process. The client told my colleague, "Charlie is not interested in me. He is only looking for names that I can provide." Even though this connection was set up by my colleague and the client agreed to facilitate this endeavor, I did not follow the process. I did not get to know my audience, nor did I establish a relationship with him. This backfired.

Let's talk about **Crossing That Sales Bridge...BEFORE We Get There.**

Planning

Before we sit with a new customer, we need to do some research and some basic planning. At the end of the day, there are others who can provide the same product we do. The only difference is in our customer service and the additional value that we provide. What kind of information do we need to research?

1. How big is the company you are calling on? Where are the opportunities?

2. From whom are they currently buying the product that you desire to sell? Are there quality or delivery issues?

3. How does the competitor's product compare to your product? What are the weaknesses of the competitor's product? What are the strengths of your product? How do you compare price-wise? Do you need to sell on price or can you sell on value?

Understanding the customer, your competitor, and their product as it compares to yours is vital. Understanding the strengths of your company is a must if you are going to effectively solve a problem for the customer. It is time to plan your approach.

Below are listed some examples of possible ways we can solve problems:

1. **Customer is having delivery issues:** Does your company have shorter lead times or available capacity? Or does your company practice LEAN manufacturing that will allow you to design an inventory management system or a cell concept that will solve a problem for your customer?

2. **Customer is having quality issues:** Does your company have a quality management system in place? Is there additional value that you can add by testing or by providing certifications?

3. **Customer could benefit from improved quality and delivery:** Can you match the quality and deliveries at a better price? Are they satisfied with the customer service from current vendor? Does your customer have to transport freight a long distance due to the location of current vendor? If so, perhaps you can save them freight cost and shorten their lead time. Is your company willing to set up consignment inventory?

4. **Customer has to purchase many items from many suppliers and assemble them in-house:** Can you add value by providing all of the items and performing the assembly of the products for the customer?

5. **Customer needs inspecting and repackaging:** Can you package the product, put the customer's label on the box, and drop ship directly to his customer?

6. **Customer needs better pricing:** One has to be careful with getting into a price war. If you get the job because

you are the lowest priced, you will lose the business to the next company that has lower prices. Here is a thought: If the customer is sophisticated enough to provide a forecast, perhaps you can offer him a quantity price break, order more raw materials at a time, produce in higher quantity, gain some economies of scale, and provide a good price and excellent deliveries. With this kind of commitment, maybe you can negotiate a long-term agreement. I would not try to be the cheapest, because the service you are providing adds value. If you are adding value, you are increasing your internal costs.

These are the kinds of questions we need to ask and answer in our planning time. This is by no means exhaustive. Always seek to add value and solve a problem. Just as planning is important to communication, it is also important to our sales presentations.

Let's talk about customer service for a moment.

My Soap Box

There are things that frustrate us. I am going to vent for a moment. See if any of these resonate with you.

It frustrates me when I pull through a drive-in at a fast food restaurant; the teller puts the dollar bills and the receipt in my hand...and then proceeds to dump the change on top of the slippery dollars. Why can't they put the change in my hand and allow me to dump it before handing me the dollars and the receipt? There are a few that actually use manners and hand me the change first. They get my business even if I have to pay a little more. They add value to me by using common manners.

It frustrates me when I pump gas, and I get a message that I have to go inside to get my receipt. I understand the machine running out of paper, but when it happens to me three days later at the same pump, it becomes a lack of customer service. I find another station.

It frustrates me when I walk into the convenience store to get my receipt and when I leave, I stay to the right as is standard in America, push on the door to open it, and it is locked. There is no sign and no reason to keep one door locked.

It frustrates me to have to use a card at the grocery store to keep from getting gouged. Then, when I buy a pack of gum, I get a receipt that is 24 inches long!

It frustrates me when I call the parts house and can't get anyone to answer the phone. And when they do, they put me on hold and never get back to me. But when I go to the parts house in person, I can't get waited on because all the workers are on the phones. They have too few workers and they do not separate the phone business from the walk-in business. I am still looking for a parts house that knows what customer service is.

If frustrates me…and my customers when we call and get a computer system that takes us in circles.

It frustrates me...and my customers when we call, get a receptionist, ask to speak to a particular individual, and get sent directly to that individual's voicemail. Then we call back to find out if the person is even in the office today. The receptionist sends us right back to the voicemail instead of answering our question.

It frustrates me...and my customers when we have something on order and we do not find out it is going to be late until after it is late and we call to check status.

So, are there some frustrations with the new client that you can remove? It is our job to find out what is keeping the customer up at night and to remove that for him. Again, with good customer service, we add value.

Golden Nugget: The only thing that separates you from your competitors is customer service and the value you add.

Emotional Intelligence and Authenticity

Emotional Intelligence (EI) and Authenticity are the pillars of success in sales. This cannot be faked, nor can it be disguised in technique. EI and Authenticity will ensure you make a connection and position yourself to close, but this does not replace the planning.

Emotional Intelligence: The ability to assess and control the emotions of oneself, of others, and of groups. It requires astute listening to what is said and to what is only communicated through body language and facial expressions.

<u>Authenticity</u>: Worthy of acceptance or belief.

As we talk about best practices, we will talk about EI and Authenticity as well.

People with EI are self-aware, they have great self-control, they are patient, they have the ability to identify and understand others, and they exhibit great social skills. While we are not in the business to win a popularity contest, we must be likable. I had a customer tell me in regards to another company and their saleswoman that he actually gave her opportunities because he liked her and her hard work. While he was not crazy about the company she represented, he gave her as an individual opportunities anyway.

Respecting the Customer

When sitting with a customer or even calling a customer on the phone, it is vital that we fit into their schedule and that we take cues from them. When calling, always ask, "Did I catch you at a good time?" If they are on their way to a meeting and another time is better, they will tell you. If you call and immediately start talking, and you do not give them a chance to tell you that this is not a good time, they will be frustrated and resentful. I can tell you that folks are really appreciative when we respect their time and schedules.

When visiting with the customer, always be Authentic. We are trained to look for something in the customer's office to use as an ice breaker. It could be a picture of their family, some indication of their hobby, or just how organized they are. This is good...if it is Authentic. People are not stupid. Remember the used car salesman who you did not trust. He was more interested in making his commission, vomiting his sales pitch, and utilizing all the fancy sales techniques that he has in his repertoire. If he turned you off, don't emulate him and repeat his blunder.

We spoke earlier about excellence being a habit and not an act. If being genuinely interested in people is something we practice habitually, then we can authenticate it. If it is something we don't practice in our everyday lives, then it will be an act and obvious to the customer. It cannot be authenticated and it will be highly awkward.

This reminds me of Eddie Haskell on *Leave it to Beaver*. As the scene plays out, Eddie is trying to talk Wally into doing something that Wally's parents would not approve of and in walks Mrs. Cleaver. Immediately Eddie would say, "Hello. Mrs. Cleaver. That sure is a lovely dress you are wearing." Mrs. Cleaver just rolled her eyes. She saw right through the fact that he was patronizing her and there was nothing Authentic about his communication and praise.

> *"What you are speaks so loudly I can't hear what you're saying."* Ralph Waldo Emerson

Always be Authentic. People are not stupid. It is important that you make a connection in your opening and greeting time.

Whether we are giving a speech, a presentation, or going on a sales call, we need a great opening that grabs the attention of our audience and introduces our theme. The big difference between a speech and a sales call is that in spite of all of our preparation (the part of the equation you control), the delivery on a sales call is very impromptu. You have to adjust and modify your delivery on the fly because there are so many dynamics. The fact of the matter is that you have to uncover the opportunities. If they are there, you have to prospect for them. The commonality of a speech and a sales call is that you are competing for the attention of the audience.

Practice getting to know your audience. Ask questions. Remember, the one who ask questions is the one who controls the conversation. The person with EI will be able to ask enough sincere questions to find out what resonates. Remember the example of Columbo, who asked questions and get people to talking until they incriminated themselves. The same thing happens on a sales call. When people talk, they will give you the data you need to tailor your presentation.

When the customer is talking about their jobs, invariably they will say something like, *"My biggest frustration is when there is a late delivery and the vendor never bothers to notify me in advance. I don't know until the delivery is late and I call them."* This is a good time to ask more questions, such as, "Do you have to deal with this a lot?" This encourages them to keep talking. Another great question might be, "Why are the deliveries late? Have you substantially increased your demand or does the vendor have a capacity issue?" This is also a good time to empathize with your audience; *"I can see why you would be frustrated. You have made commitments to production and since you were not notified, you were not able notify your internal customer."* Now you are relating. You are meeting this customer on common ground. At this point, it becomes a very natural conversation.

You may be saying, "Charlie, this goes with being in sales. Everyone knows this." You would think so, but I have seen seasoned sales folks in action and wonder how they have made a career in sales.

When you have planned and created a sales kit filled with solutions and value, and you carry this kit on the back of authenticity and emotional intelligence, engage both of your listening ears, respect the customer's time and exercise flexibility on your delivery, then you ready for a WIN and long-term Sustainable Success in Sales.

If you jump in with a sales pitch right off the bat, I promise you the customer is tuning out. Save the pitch for later after you and your client come up with the right material together. If you do a good enough job of solving the problems and adding value, the customer might even provide the sales pitch as to why you should allow them to buy from you.

Also respect people's time when you are in their presence. If you see the customer looking at his watch, it is time to start winding down. If the customer gets really talkative, you may want to ask what his time constraints are. You have to be ready to say, "I know you are busy, so I will wrap it up."

Golden Nugget: People embrace the person before they embrace the pitch.

Respect the time of your client. Be authentic and genuine. If this is awkward, practice in your daily life. How do we practice being authentic and genuine? When you are visiting with friends, speaking with your spouse, or meeting with your clients, make a deliberate effort to be interested and to show interest. Ask questions that you know are related to their interests and REALLY listen to the answers. You will find that this will energize you while making a real connection with your audience. Here is a simple piece of advice: If someone comes to your office to see you, take your hands and eyes off of your phone and computer and look at the person vying for your attention.

Spend the time planning by understanding the customer, his products, and your competition. At the same time, be an expert on what your company does well and be knowledgeable of industrial strategies that your company could implement to win a new customer. With proper planning, you will be patient, you will be a proactive listener, and you will be flexible on the delivery of your pitch.

Having done all you can to plan, it is time to create the Picture of your Successful Pitch.

Picturing the Successful Pitch

I am convinced that we can worry and fear a thing into existence. It is called a self-fulfilling prophecy. We spoke in Chapter 4 about focusing on something until our minds develop the picture and then our bodies will turn it into a motion picture. If that which we focus on is worry, fear, or failing, it too will come to pass.

Golden Nugget: Worry and Fear fertilize weeds.

Creating a picture where everyone is relaxed, there is joking and smiling, and all are glad to see one another is far more effective than allowing the worry weeds to overtake our minds.

On one of my recent trips to Singapore, I had the pleasure of visiting a troubled customer. Let me explain. An upset customer is an opportunity to be a problem-solver and to be a hero in their eyes. The majority of the existing problems are out of our control. We ship the same product all over the world, but in Singapore, they get rejected. The QC Manager, my sales engineer, and I teamed up to visit this customer.

As we sat at lunch and went over the PowerPoint presentation, I took the time to prepare the QC Manager on the subtle differences of the Asian culture. For instance, they will not interrupt the presentation to ask a question, even if you invite them to do so. This is considered rude. You have to stop and ask if there are questions.

As our QC Manager took us through the presentation, I

asked questions as if I were the customer. This helped us to catch culture and language inconsistencies and plan for where we needed to expound or where different language would be more appropriate. We were not sure what we were walking into, so we made the decision to walk in with big smiles and a lot of energy. We pictured being happy to see them and vice versa. This turned out to be a great meeting. It should have, because that is how we pictured it. We made the conscious decision to set the tone for the meeting through the picture we created. In fact, we practiced smiling while en route to see the customer.

> *"A smile says, I like you. You make me happy. And I am glad to see you."* Dale Carnegie

If you have done a good job of planning and anticipated the hard questions and objections, and you have a great grip on your responses, then you need to picture yourself as relaxed, smiling, and confident when answering tough questions. Many times we are not comfortable with some of our answers, and we consider them a stretch or weak. If we do not believe in them, neither will our customers. Picture success in presenting these responses. Keep your answers truth-based and step up to the plate and commit. Last but not least, we need to be clear on our purpose. We need to know why we are pushing forward.

Creating or Finding Purpose in a Sales Call

Do you remember that purpose creates passion and passion creates energy? What is your purpose for being in sales? It is to be a problem-solver! It is adding value! It is making frustrations go away! It is rescuing a poor little customer from a big, bad, mean, and underperforming vendor! Do you agree? I am doing that salesman technique again, aren't I?

The better job you do at understanding and being an expert on what separates your company and your products from your competitors, the more confident you will be as a problem-solver. As you gain this expertise, you will find purpose in being a crusader for companies that need to be rescued from mediocre vendors.

As you identify those qualities that separate your company, you also realize where you add value and can command a higher margin for the company. It does cost money for company to maintain engineers, chemists, an R&D Lab, a quality management system, LEAN directors, training, and programs to ensure a flawless, quality product. There is nothing wrong with providing additional value, solving a problem for the customer, removing frustrations, and getting paid for that service.

It is my desire that I have shared some ideas to help you to be all that you were created to be. If someday our paths cross and you tell me that you received one idea that motivated you to move closer to your dreams, then the time invested in writing this book will pale in comparison to the joy I will receive.

Always **Cross That Bridge...BEFORE You Get There**. Invest time in preparation. Plan your activities and approach. Paint the Picture of what Success looks like. And always find or create Purpose in everything you do.

You were created to accomplish great things. You are here for a very specific purpose. You are a Guppy Eater!

I dispatch you to go forth and achieve.

It is now that time to tell you what my boss loves to tell me: "Go Sell Something!"

Golden Nuggets and Quotes

- "You don't close a sale, you open a relationship if you want to build a long-term, successful enterprise." Patricia Fripp

- "Most people think 'selling' is the same as 'talking.' But the most effective salespeople know that listening is the most important part of their job." Roy Bartell

- People embrace the person before they embrace the pitch.

- Worry and fear fertilize weeds.

- "What you are speaks so loudly I can't hear what you're saying." Ralph Waldo Emerson

- The only thing that separates you from your competitors is customer service and the value you add.

Notes Page:

Reference	Page No.

The End

And Hopefully, A New Beginning!

I would also like to leave you with a short list of books that have truly inspired and helped me.

Books on People Skills & Leadership:

How to Win Friends and Influence People, Dale Carnegie

Developing the Leader Within You, John C. Maxwell

Developing the Leaders Around You, John Maxwell

The Peter Principle, Peter Raymond Hull

Books on Success & Self- Improvement:

Failing Forward, John C. Maxwell

The Purpose Driven Life, Rick Warren

The Search For Significance, Robert S. McGee

What to Say When You Talk to Yourself, Shad Helmsetter

Seven Habits of Highly Effective People, Steven Covey

The Anatomy of an Illness, Norman Cousins

Developing Self-Confidence & Influencing People by Public Speaking, Dale Carnegie

Success Through Positive Mental Attitude, Norman Vincent Peale and W. Clement Stone

Everyone Communicates, Few Connect, John C. Maxwell

Books on Financial Success:

The Millionaire Next Door, Thomas Stanly and William D. Danko

Think and Grow Rich, Norman Vincent Peale

Financial Peace. Dave Ramsey

Books on Sales:

The Greatest Salesman in the World, Og Mandino

24 Closings, Brian Tracey

The Psychology of Selling, Brian Tracey

Million Dollar Habits, Brian Tracey

Getting to Yes, Negotiating Agreement Without Giving In, Robert Fisher and William Ury

Books on Excellence in Business:

The Goal, Eliyahu M. Goldratt

Good to Great, Jim Collins

Built to Last, Jim Collins

Fish, Stephen C. Laudin , Harry Paul and Christensen

Who Moved my Cheese, Spencer Johnson

Charlie Pitts is a motivational speaker delivering a great balance of inspiration and information.

If you are looking for a keynote speaker for your event or some motivational training to bring your team up a notch, Charlie delivers.

For questions, you can contact Mr. Pitts at:
charlie@charliepitts.com
Home Page: www.charliepitts.com
Blog: www.successbridge.wordpress.com
Twitter: www.twitter.com/charliepitts4

20154071R00079

Made in the USA
Charleston, SC
28 June 2013